CALAMITY JANE

CALAMITY JANE

The Life and Legend of Martha Jane Cannary

D. J. HERDA

TWODOT®

GUILFORD, CONNECTICUT

A · TWODOT® · BOOK

An imprint of The Rowman & Littlefield Publishing Group, Inc.
4501 Forbes Blvd., Ste. 200
Lanham, MD 20706

A registered trademark of The Rowman & Littlefield Publishing Group, Inc.

Distributed by NATIONAL BOOK NETWORK

British Library Cataloguing in Publication Information available

Library of Congress Cataloging-in-Publication Data

Names: Herda, D. J., 1948- author.
Title: Calamity Jane : the life and legend of Martha Jane Cannary / D. J. Herda.
Other titles: Life and legend of Martha Jane Cannary
Description: Guilford, Connecticut : TwoDot, [2018] | Includes bibliographical references.
Identifiers: LCCN 2017057179| ISBN 9781493031948 (pap : alk. paper) | ISBN 9781493031955 (e-book)
Subjects: LCSH: Calamity Jane, 1856-1903. | Women pioneers—West (U.S.)—Biography. | Pioneers—West (U.S.)—Biography. | West (U.S.)—Biography.
Classification: LCC F594.C2 H47 2018 | DDC 978/.02092 [B] —dc23 LC record available at https://lccn.loc.gov/2017057179

♾™ The paper used in this publication meets the minimum requirements of American National Standard for Information Sciences—Permanence of Paper for Printed Library Materials, ANSI/NISO Z39.48-1992.

Printed in the United States of America

CONTENTS

Introduction

THEY SAY THE TRUTH SHALL SET YOU FREE. BUT, IN THE CASE OF A woman named Calamity, they're wrong. It's true that she recorded the details of her own life, a rare gift left behind for biographers over which to salivate. But biographers do *not* salivate over this subject. Instead, they scratch their heads and tell us that her own words are an aberration of the truth. The words are little more than so much publicity feeding into the persona of someone who called herself Calamity Jane—someone who never really existed. Not as she had documented. Her words were more Legend than Truth.

But what is truth and what is legend and how does each contribute to the historical accuracy of a biographical figure taken from the pages of time?

It's true: Calamity's legend, it would appear, precedes her. But not the reality.

Or *does* it?

A legend springs up around a body; it's not a lifeless cosmic entity *created* by it. And certainly Calamity Jane had seen her share of legends spring up around her. From books written about her. Newspaper articles. Magazine stories. Wild West shows. Gossipy neighbors. Tall tales passed from one generation to the next.

Some of them are undeniably true. Some are false. When looking through the life and times of Calamity Jane, nothing is as it appears. Was she born in 1852, as she claimed, or 1856? In Princeton, Missouri, as she said, or the hinterlands of Ohio? Did she ride with Generals Crook, Miles, and Custer? Was she on the Newton-Jenney Expedition into the Badlands of South Dakota to confirm rumors of massive deposits of precious gold? Did she know Wild Bill Hickok intimately, casually, or not at all? Was she the gilt-edged Florence Nightingale of the American Plains or the devil incarnate?

Her biographers agree to disagree. They present proof that disputes her own written accounts of her life's events. But even that evidence is subject to human error and misinterpretation.

So, in the end, we are left with Martha Jane's own words of her life's history. And with the legends. And that can be both good and bad.

Legends can be misleading. But they are a necessary part of nation-building. They are the primary means we have of preserving the seeds of reality that sprout into something larger than life and grow under the weight of their own dominion. Legends must contain truth to flourish, or else they will wither and die before ever having had a chance to take root. As they grow, they become permanently affixed in our minds. Like Pocahontas saving the life of Jamestown's John Smith or the Chesapeake & Ohio's John Henry, that "steel-drivin' man," who went toe-to-toe with a steam-powered hammer and won.

As far as Calamity Jane goes, who would have recalled without the aid of legend that she ever even *knew* Wild Bill Hickok? Who would have remembered that she slept with him, fought alongside him, loved him, nurtured him through the pipe, "married" him, bore him a child, set him free so that he could marry another, wept for him at his gravesite, and vowed to bring his murdering assassin Jack McCall to justice? Which of us, in fact—but for the legends surrounding her—would know *any* of her life's story, the true and the false, the good and the bad? Would you have recalled that she at least *knew* Wild Bill and loved him even if none of the other legends swirling around her relationship to him had come to pass?

Probably not.

Legends are stories we build within our minds. Like highways, they carry travelers from one spot to another. In that sense, legends are reality on steroids. Although they may be exaggerations of the truth, they help us to understand the reality a little more clearly through our own historical perspectives. If legends enable us to do that, how bad can they be?

In the end, legends are created by storytellers who, in weaving their craft, expose themselves as gossipers and lie mongers and prevaricators and feasting jackals via their tales. If Calamity were alive today, she would agree that she was a damn first-rate storyteller on her own . . . and be proud of it.

Of course, she was no gilded lily. Far from it. Calamity herself would have admitted there had been some reporters who referred to her over the years as a drunk and a whore and an outright liar and a blasphemer and a gambler and a common thief. To those people, she would have said, *Guilty as charged!* After all, she recognized early in life that a gal has to build a reputation for herself if she's going to remain in demand and survive in a hostile world dominated by hostile men. And Calamity Jane remained in demand and survived for more than half a century.

Over the course of these past hundred-plus years since her passing, the restless spirit of Calamity Jane has walked the sagging boards and dusty trails of life, waiting for her story to be told. Her own life's story from the recollections of the woman herself—Calamity Jane. It is the truth as Calamity knew it—or at least *believed* it—to be true. It is the truth varnished with the tint of legend that created from her earliest recollections the Woman-Child she eventually turned out to be. Taller than real life and yet smaller than death.

Whether accurate or exaggerated, this is the story of Martha Jane Cannary's life, as she lived it, saw it, and hoped it to be remembered. Only a select few people had the opportunity to write down her words and actions and feelings and thoughts as they unfolded. And maybe to fill in a little between the cracks for those parts of the legend Calamity may have overlooked.

But only one of those people was named Calamity Jane. Only one of them left a roadmap of the life she led as a notorious plainswoman. Only one of them wrote her autobiography and stepped back to dare others following in her footsteps to claim it untrue or exaggerated—which, of course, many biographers have done.

But Calamity Jane's story is not one to which a traditional historical biography can do justice. Thus was born this book, the historical enactment of the life Calamity Jane wanted us to believe she lived—and perhaps herself believed she had lived. Judging her through the lens of the psychohistorian who has studied her throughout time, this book offers new insights into the woman Calamity worked so hard to create and assign to the pages of history. For that, she is to be remembered and applauded. A liar? A charlatan? A scoundrel? A brigand? Or was she merely a product of her environment—as are we all—and of her circumstances? If so, given the harsh realities she was forced to face from her earliest days on earth, it is a miracle she had any ego left at all by the time she passed from it.

While most of the dialogues contained within are historically documented, some are psychohistorically recreated. All are in keeping with Calamity's own presentation of and beliefs about herself, her family, and her life. As such, they shed valuable light on the probability of what the real Martha Jane Cannary was like—long before she had a chance to morph into the free-spirited character known as Calamity Jane.

As such, this is the only portrait of Calamity created from her own words—directly or indirectly, remembered correctly, overlooked, taken from sources who knew her, historically psychoanalyzed from afar, dissected from up close, or even long since ignored or forgotten. These are *her* words about *her* life as she *intended* them to be told—recalled accurately or implied, embellished or shot straight from the hip like a .38-caliber revolver fired from the back of a charging steed in Buffalo Bill's Wild West Show.

Exactly as things happened.

Or, at least, as far as she wanted us to know.

CHAPTER ONE

Calamity: An Autobiography

A woman who has killed more than five score of Indians, who has met and conquered a dozen bad men, and has been in more deadly rows than falls to the lot of a hundred average men, is now earning a living as a book agent.
—BURLINGTON GAZETTE, NOVEMBER 17, 1896

THE RUGGED, POROUS LANDS OF THE BLACK HILLS-TO-LARAMIE ROAD couldn't have been more inviting. The coach, clattering along the trail, called out to everyone within hundreds of miles: *Take me, I'm yours.*

And one day, after waylaying that very same stage only weeks earlier and making off with sixty thousand dollars in gold and cash, one group of men attempted it again. As the driver urged the eight-horse team around the bend, half a dozen killers armed to the teeth poured down on them from the rocky hillside. Releasing a volley of shots, one of the outlaws hit the driver in the chest. He slumped forward, turning to his sidekick and handing off the reins.

"I'm hit," he called, clutching his chest. "I'm hit bad. Don't let 'em get *you*, Marthy. Run 'em back to town."

Martha Jane Cannary grabbed the reins and, as she had done so many times before, whistled to the team, whipping them into a frenzy. With hot lead zinging past her, Martha poured on the fuel; and when the first outlying facades of Deadwood loomed just over the horizon, she breathed her first deep breath in a lifetime.

The gunshots slowed in pace, their sounds diminishing sharply. As the coach poured into town and people came running out to see about the clatter, the outlaws stopped, turned, and rode off once more into the hills that sheltered them from the law.

Martha pulled the team up in front of the depot, checked on her companion, and climbed down from the seat. The sheriff came running out of his office just as the first of the coach's six passengers emerged unscathed.

"What is it? What happened here?"

Martha shook the dust from her sleeves, looking back over her shoulder.

"Holdup," she said, motioning with her head. "'Fraid poor ol' Jack's made his last run."

That was only one of the experiences Martha Jane Cannary—aka Calamity Jane—wrote about in her autobiography in 1896. Or, rather, she *had* written about her. Approaching the end of her fourth decade on earth, Calamity was illiterate; she had to hire a ghostwriter to scribe her life into a pamphlet. Short life: shorter pamphlet.

Once her autobiography was complete, she had a local printer publish copies for her to sell to anyone who seemed a likely customer. Which meant anyone who had ever heard anything at all about Calamity Jane or talked with her for an hour or two on the streets or—more likely—in the saloons. Calamity had learned early that living such a colorful life while having been born a female was an advantage few other women her age could claim. She realized she would have been foolish not to press every advantage—and she did just that.

Now, many people who write about themselves do so out of an overblown sense of superiority. Jane did not. She published and sold copies of her life's story out of a need to survive, *period.* By the time she had reached her fourth decade of life on earth, she was an aging, sickly, compassionate, unemployed drunk. And even *colorful* drunks have to have a way of earning enough money to keep them off the wagon. The decision was no more complicated than that.

When she was younger, she had far more opportunities to walk into a saloon and, inside of a few hours, play a few hands of poker, win a game or two of faro, and buy a round for the house. That naturally led to the house buying a few rounds for her. She was, after all, the notorious Calamity Jane. It didn't take her long to figure out the odds involved in *that* one.

But as she grew older and longer of tooth, her looks, which when she was young and "dressed to the nines," were girl-next-door *attractive*, turned to being ruggedly mannish. Her squared-off jaw, steely blue eyes, and high Choctaw cheekbones began to change. Under the strain of a harsh wilderness life, they morphed into a fleeting image of what they had been once. The men stopped courting her, stopped lavishing money on her, stopped paying her to go to bed with them. And her natural instincts at scouting and Indian fighting and running with the miners off to the next gold or silver strike soon abandoned her, much the same way her mother had done by dying so young of age in her own life. Before long, Calamity found herself in declining health and poor finances and—more often than not—*alone*. And, if truth be known, just a little afraid.

Enter Calamity with her autobiography, which she had inked for very several specific reasons. For one, Calamity Jane had only recently begun appearing in Wild West shows and exhibitions back East. What better way to hype her popularity with her audiences than to tout her personal accomplishments and experiences—even if exaggerated? Who hadn't heard of George Armstrong Custer and wouldn't be impressed if Jane revealed she had ridden with him as a scout on his Indian campaigns throughout the West?

Another reason was to keep some of her friends and neighbors anxious to rub elbows with her at the bar—and, of course, to pick up the tab. Who wouldn't want to admit he had shared time with the one-and-only Calam on more than one occasion? And drunk with her, played cards with her, or simply knew her on a first-name basis?

For those people and all the people everywhere who had heard the name but never knew it belonged to a real person, they could tell their friends and family: *I knew Calamity Jane when.*

Who's Calamity Jane? Some of them might have asked.

Here, now. Some of them might have replied. *Here's Calamity Jane, in this pamphlet right here where you can read all about her for yourself in her very own words. And remember this: I wuz her friend!*

Or not.

CHAPTER TWO

A Family Affair

My maiden name was Marthy Cannary; was born in Princeton, Mo., May 1, 1852; father and mother natives of Ohio; had two brothers and three sisters, I being the oldest of the children.
—THE AUTOBIOGRAPHY OF CALAMITY JANE

LOCAL MERCER COUNTY, MISSOURI, LAND RECORDS DATING FROM THE death of Martha Jane's grandfather, James Cannary, show the family had only recently moved to Princeton, Missouri, from their ancestral home in Ohio, arriving in 1856. Grandpa James was a tough bird, a hard-nosed yet fair-minded self-made man who lived life the only way he knew how: full out.

He arrived in Missouri with his son, Robert, and Robert's wife, Charlotte, in late April. Charlotte was pregnant during the trip, and Martha Jane was born only two days after her grandpa had settled the family in with them and bought some land.

For one reason or another, the Cannary family patriarch didn't hold onto his new acquisition for long. Shortly after buying the land, he began selling it off for considerably less than the $1,775 he had just paid for it—not exactly a shrewd business deal.

He sold forty acres to Robert Southers, one of his sons-in-law, for fifty dollars in 1856 and followed that up with one hundred acres for four hundred dollars to another son-in-law, James Kilgore, three years later. Southers and Kilgore were married to Robert's sisters, Martha's aunts, Lana and Mary. Divesting himself of his holdings, Grandpa James sold the remaining 180 acres of his land for five hundred dollars to Robert and Charlotte. After Grandpa James's wife, Sarah, died, James retired and lived with Robert, Charlotte, and his precious new granddaughter, Martha Jane, for the remainder of his days.

When Grandpa James passed away on June 30, 1862, he willed his holdings to be split among his nine children, the heirs to his estate. Robert and three of his siblings, Mary, Lana, and brother James Thornton (called "Thornton" to avoid confusion with their father), were living in Missouri at the time.

Although the Mercer County land that James and his wife had bought boasted no major rivers, it did have numerous rolling valleys with several small creeks and idyllic streams carving their way through them, surrounded by elm, hickory, ash, and beech trees that provided both free building materials and fuel for the icy midwestern winters. Expanses of open fields offered rich, fertile farmland, as well as green pasture for grazing livestock. Early farmers in the area grew corn, oats, wheat, and hay, plus the occasional tobacco, potatoes, and sorghum for molasses. Mercer County's remote location accounted for its slow growth. The continuing issue of slavery also played a part in the failure of the population explosion to make itself known.

But the paucity of the population combined with the rural nature of the area suited the elder Cannary just fine. Patriarch James had come from a sparsely populated part of Ohio in Monroe County with a population of only 2,691 in 1850. Princeton, the Missouri County seat, remained an unincorporated boondocks until 1853.

Grandpa James's son and daughter-in-law, Robert and Charlotte, lived with him and James's wife, Sarah, at their Missouri home for several months. The house where Martha Jane took her first breath was a large log building with several rooms upstairs, a common style of home for its day.

Although James Cannary wasn't exactly wealthy, he was far from poor. The 1862 probate court's list of personal property left behind after his death showed that his holdings included three horses (one a mare with a colt); a pair of oxen; three cows with calves; a yearling steer; a yearling heifer; eleven sheep; and twelve hogs. In addition to the livestock, James owned two wagons; a plow; a long-handled shovel; a breakfast table; two bedsteads; two feather beds; a stove; a chest; a windmill; a sausage grinder; and other miscellaneous items. Interestingly enough, given the fact that he was illiterate, he nonetheless owned a family bible and "one large Testament."

Meanwhile, James's daughter-in-law, Charlotte—a wild woman of indomitable spirit, much to the endless chagrin of her husband, Robert—often shocked their Princeton, Missouri, neighbors with her behavior, which included cigar smoking, drinking, and cursing. One day, after she had spent more than her share of time at the local saloon, she hopped aboard the family buggy and rode past a neighbor's home with some red calico. As the spinster woman came out to see what all the racket was about, Charlotte flung the cloth at the woman's feet, chiding her to "take that and make a dress for your damn bastard!"

Robert was tolerated ever so slightly more. Despite a reputation for being a lazy sloth (the cog driving all the family's incompetence), his real estate and personal property were listed in the 1860 census at fifteen hundred dollars and four hundred dollars respectively, quite a bit more than those of his nearby and "more industrious" brother-in-law, James Kilgore, which were listed at three hundred dollars and four hundred dollars, on par with the estates of most of their neighbors. Robert, according to many of his countrymen, did the best he could for his children, who apparently turned out fairly well—at least while the parents were alive. One descendant of the times, Mrs. Elijah Pickett, recalled Martha as being "a nice child who played with the Pickett children" often. Martha Jane may even have had some schooling. Although she didn't attend for long, several local histories suggest that she once was enrolled in a local "subscription school"—a school that charged families a subscription fee to educate their children. Private schools, along with various entrepreneurial and denominational institutions, emerged about the same time, mostly in larger towns and cities, and received public funds. Subscription schools were primarily "sink or swim" so far as funding went. Often, they existed one day and went belly up the next.

Martha Jane never received much schooling at home either, since her mother, Charlotte, was illiterate, as were Grandpa James and Aunts Lana and Mary.

The years before the Cannarys left Missouri were troublesome for the family. Relations between the Northern and Southern states had escalated to crisis stage. Charlotte was a "Secesh," or a Confederate sympathizer, who rarely saw eye to eye with her pro-Union neighbors, although Thornton Cannary, who remained in Missouri throughout the Civil War, apparently had no problems with his neighbors despite his brief enlistment in the state militia in 1861, when Missouri allied with the Confederacy.

But rather than leave Missouri because of escalating political pressures the way so many families did, the Cannary family headed off to "the goldfields of Montana," where they hoped to strike it rich after rich veins of the ore were discovered there at Alder Gulch.

That meant one thing for certain for Robert, Charlotte, Martha Jane, and her younger siblings, Lena and Cilus: The family's dynamics were about to change.

Forever.

CHAPTER THREE

Wagons Ho!

In 1865 we migrated by overland route to Virginia City, Mont.; took five months for this journey. While on the way the greater portion of my time was spent in hunting along with the men. In fact I was at all times along with the men when there was excitement or adventure to be had.

—THE AUTOBIOGRAPHY OF CALAMITY JANE

CILUS DIED IN HIS SLEEP IN 1862. NO ONE EVER KNEW WHY. ONE NIGHT he went to bed as always, and the next morning he failed to awaken. Charlotte wept and sobbed and wailed hysterically—couldn't stop, couldn't *breathe*, she cried so hard. Martha, still a child herself, said she'd ride for the doctor; but Robert—tears in his eyes, head bowed low—knew better.

It was the darkest period of the Cannarys' lives together, the most horrible days any of the family had ever known. But after a few weeks had passed, Charlotte had an announcement to make. She was pregnant. One child lost and another found. One son gone and another ready to take its place. This one, she and her husband had decided to name Elijah, or Lige for short.

With the good times back once more, Robert packed up his wife and three children—Martha, Lena, and baby Elijah—and headed west to make their fortunes. They stopped in Iowa to visit with Charlotte's family before embarking on the remainder of the journey to the goldfields of Montana.

Years later, Martha learned the real reason for the family's sudden departure from Missouri. Her father had "borrowed" several hundred dollars from a trust fund set up by his father, Grandpa James, for the benefit of all the brothers and sisters. Somehow Robert had forgotten to pay the money back. As a result, a court order demanded his appearance before the county magistrate to provide an accounting of those missing funds, as well as the resolution of several additional issues involving some mislaid stocks, bonds, and other valuables that seemed to have evaporated with his father's death. Upon being served with a legal complaint, Robert took only days to convince his wife that the time couldn't have been more propitious to pursue a change of venue—forwarding address unknown!

So, pooling their meager savings and buying their way onto a small wagon train, the family hit the trail. Martha was ecstatic. Besides feeding her already adventurous spirit, the additional tasks her father faced of driving a wagon while caring for the livestock and watching over his family kept him occupied to the point of being forced to loosen the reins on his eldest daughter. In turn, Martha, already an accomplished rider while in Missouri, became an even more highly skilled horsewoman on the journey. Taller, heftier, larger boned, and more outgoing than other girls her age, she quickly grew to be accepted by the scouts and drivers on the train as "one of the boys." During the trip, Martha later recalled, she became a "remarkable good shot and fearless rider for a girl of my age." Hanging out with the men on the train, how could she not?

To the other members of the train, Martha's parents must have presented the ultimate concept of "strange." Those who remembered them from their years in Missouri farm country recounted Robert as a relatively sober, unassuming man, quietly ineffective at the prerequisite task of making a living. Charlotte, some fifteen years his junior, was fond of dressing in colorful clothing and expressing her opinions in equally flamboyant language. There was little doubt from which side of the family Martha had gotten her spirit!

Although the Cannarys had been short of both funding and experience before setting out on their cross-country journey, they managed to persevere through the five-month trip. When their travels finally drew to a close, they found themselves deposited on the doorstep of Nevada City, Montana, where they occupied a makeshift cabin, and Robert quickly turned his attention to panning and rooting around the rolling foothills for gold.

Nevada City was the perfect place for the Cannary family patriarch to settle in. Throughout the 1860s, miners—both real and wannabe—flooded the western part of Montana with its initial findings and widespread rumors of new strikes bringing a stampede of men with picks and shovels to the Front Range. The endless stream of migrations west most often targeted Montana's Bannock, Nevada City, Alder Gulch/Virginia City, Last Chance Gulch, Helena, and Confederate Gulch/Diamond City. All these areas fell siege to the glint-eyed prospectors—some, like the Cannarys, with their families in tow. They created a burgeoning strain on the resources of the minuscule communities, many of which exploded in population overnight. Five thousand immigrants crowded into Alder Gulch/Virginia City alone within the first six months of news of a strike. And why not? That ten-mile stretch of rolling lush mountain land gave up thirty *million* dollars in the first three years alone and more than three times that amount in total! Word spread like wildfire. Before long, miners covered the hillsides with tents, brush shelters, and crude log cabins.

The area known as Alder Gulch, with its rock-strewn hillsides and wide, meandering canyon, was part of the expansion of gold mining from California into the western United States. The gold rushes of the 1860s had led Congress to create five new territories, including Alder Gulch, which was originally situated in Idaho Territory until May 1864, when it officially became part of Montana.

By mid-1864, Virginia City, the territorial capital, had become the largest of the settlements with an estimated population of more than five thousand. It soon grew to be the territory's most important social center and transportation hub.

By the time Robert Cannary and his family arrived in the area, the mining camps were already booming. The gold was there for the taking—*if* you knew where to look and how to go about getting it.

Robert didn't.

Before long, the family fell upon even harder times than it had left behind in Missouri. When winter snows blanketed the canyon beginning in late autumn, the mammoth drifts formed an impenetrable blockage, making food scarce. Baby Lige cried for lack of milk. Lena grew thin, losing nearly a quarter of her weight in one month. Martha—well, she was Martha and never complained once. Instead, she went out on the hunt nearly every day, often returning with *something* the family could turn into a meal, no matter how meager.

But while the availability of meat was a given, vegetables and other foodstuffs were rare. Flour sold for $1.50 a pound—an extravagant price that no one except those few prospectors who had already struck it rich could afford to pay. Vegetables—fresh, in particular, but even dried—were nearly impossible to find at *any* price. Peaches went for as much as four dollars a can!

To survive, the Cannary family focused on doing what it had always done in difficult times: struggled. Charlotte went back to work as a bar girl, taking in laundry during the day and men by night. Robert tried his hand at professional gambling—an unlikely pursuit for someone of his limited skills and dubious temperament.

Even the children joined in the hunt to escape poverty. The *Montana Post* once headlined a story on New Year's Eve, 1864: "Provision for the Destitute Poor." The tale that followed summarized the Cannary plight when it described how "three little girls, who state their names to be Cannary" appeared at the home of James Fergus, seeking aid. Fergus had been charged with the prodigious task of helping the poor in Virginia City. He never wanted for work. The newspaper article continued:

> *The father, it seems, is a gambler in Nevada [City]. The mother is a woman of the lowest grade. . . . A calico slip without any additional clothing was all that defended the poor children from the inclemency of the weather. . . . We understand that the little ones returned to Nevada [City], where they have existed for some time.*

The paper went on to lambaste the Cannary parents, describing them as "inhuman brutes who have deserted their poor unfortunate children" by displaying a "most flagrant and wanton instance of unnatural conduct" on their part.

Far from letting the story upset him, Robert turned his focus to other more lucrative reports. He concentrated on articles about a massive strike in the Ophir area north of Alder Gulch and west of Helena.

"Do you know what this means?" he likely asked his wife.

Overjoyed, she opened her eyes wide and cried, "We'll be rich!"

So, in May 1865, the Cannary family packed up their meager belongings and moved once more, this time, to nearby Blackfoot City, Montana. They weren't alone. The mad rush to get in on the strike drew boomers from across the country, swelling the area's population to two thousand inhabitants nearly overnight.

But not all went well for the Cannarys. Early in 1866, Charlotte grew inexplicably ill, her physical and mental health failing fast. Before anyone could do anything about it, she died. She was buried in the nearby cemetery—a cold, lonely, and foreboding place—without so much as a tombstone to survive her. And, just like that, the Cannary family walls came tumbling down around them once more.

Robert—desperate, jobless, and despondent—decided to uproot his children again, this time moving them to Salt Lake City, Utah, where he had heard that the Mormons in their recently established settlement had a reputation for caring for their families—and might even be persuaded to take in a few new members. But shortly after arriving in 1867, he died, bitter and beaten, leaving Martha, the oldest of the siblings, to face overwhelming new challenges on her own, not the least of which was the arduous and heartbreaking task of farming out her siblings to the neighboring polygamist families. Within several weeks, Lena and Elijah had been placed in foster homes.

It was a time of emotional stress for the girl that took a heavy toll on her and would continue to haunt her remaining days on earth. Not only was she forced to split up the family, leaving behind the brother and sister she loved so dearly, but also she was left with the haunting realization of the shortcomings of two parents that never should have had *one* child, let alone more. As Martha looked back upon life, she saw a father's frustration, declining morals, and an inability to stand up to the everyday demands of life. In her mother, she witnessed the substitution of lust-filled sex and physical attraction for respectability, marriage, and motherhood.

In light of the two most powerful influences in her life, Martha Jane Cannary, alone in a strange new world to face only God knew *what* lay ahead, was destined for failure.

The only saving grace for her was that, at the time, she didn't know it. And she never would.

CHAPTER FOUR

Love, Life, Death, and Wyoming

Remained in Utah until 1867 where my father died, then went to Fort Bridger, Wyo. Arrived May 1, 1868. Remained around Fort Bridger during 1868, then went to Piedmont, Wyo., with the U.P. railway.

—*THE AUTOBIOGRAPHY OF CALAMITY JANE*

FOLLOWING HER FATHER'S DEATH, MARTHA WANDERED THE RUTTED streets in search of small jobs. They were not easy to find. Salt Lake City, despite its moniker, was little more than a well-fortified camp of Mormon expatriates who had begun settling there only fifteen years earlier after being booted out of Palmira, New York; Nauvoo, Illinois; and other towns and settlements along the Mormon Trail west. The City at the time consisted of several two-story wood-frame and brick buildings standing guard over rutted dirt-and-clay streets. The grander of the structures vied with hastily thrown together wooden boxes and a small tent town that provided the focal point of the metropolis. Camp Davis, which was subsequently upgraded to a U.S. military fort, dominated the scenery, providing protection for the citizens, as well as for the railroad, which had laid its tracks along the Great Salt Lake to feed the burgeoning town and keep its occupants supplied with provisions shipped in from the East. Several Ute Indian families also banded together outside the fort, pitching their teepees in the hopes of enjoying the largesse the military provided in exchange for peace amid the plains.

When at last Martha grew despondent over the lack of opportunities presenting themselves for a young girl left alone and to her own devices, she left Utah and headed off to Fort Bridger, Wyoming, an outpost set among the vast rolling foothills leading to the very pinnacles of the Rocky Mountains.

Fort Bridger had been founded in order to guard stage routes and the transcontinental telegraph line. It also helped keep open a Pony Express station with its routes traveling both east and west. The Fort stood guard over several outlying towns, all the while its soldiers patrolling trails traveled by emigrants passing through the area on their way to the goldfields of California. The soldiers regularly engaged hostile Indians who raided the mining camps and small settlements along the valley comprising the South Pass and Sweetwater region, whose inhabitants were intent upon seeking their fortunes. The soldiers also helped protect and supply workers constructing the Union Pacific Railroad not far to the north.

Desperate to keep the area open to increased white settlement, the United States government in Washington signed a major treaty in 1868 with the Shoshone and the Bannock Indians, stating in part, "From this day forward peace between the parties to this treaty shall forever continue. The Government of the United States desires peace, and its honor is hereby pledged to keep it. The Indians desire peace, and they hereby pledge their honor to maintain it."

On a practical note, the treaty meant that whites could travel and settle the area without as much fear of Indian reprisals as before, although the Sioux were still present in Wyoming Territory and not yet willing to enter into any sort of agreement with the Great White Father in the East.

Martha, arriving at Fort Bridger, soon caught the eye of *everyone*. Young, girlishly attractive, outgoing, and flirtatious, she was in addition to those traits one other thing few people at the time had ever witnessed in a young female traveler: *alone!* Filled with the sort of confidence that most young girls in their mid-teens lacked, Martha Jane soon made the acquaintance of Major Patrick A. Gallagher and his wife, Fannie. The couple was amazed at Martha's high spirits despite having come from a history of such overwhelming misfortune. In time, they asked if they could "adopt" her, taking her into their family. Martha, overwhelmed at the opportunities for the spirited adventure that Wyoming held for her, leaped at the opportunity.

Before long, Gallagher, who had built a reputation for serving the local garrison with distinction, succumbed to the rumors of gold and decided to try his hand at mining. How difficult could it be? *Besides*, he must have reasoned, *if the rumors are true, gold nuggets the size of my fist lay on the ground just begging to be picked up!*

So, in the summer of 1868, Gallagher and his wife packed up their belongings and took young Martha with them to South Pass City, one of several mining camps that had recently sprouted from the wilderness. While she lived with the Gallaghers, Martha was described as "quite a nice and likable looking young woman even while she was in South Pass, but she finally ran away from them [the Gallaghers]." Addressing the notoriety that later engulfed Calamity Jane, the woman added that Martha "was not exactly wild for she was only a young girl at this time."

The reason for Martha's falling-out with the Gallaghers came to light when local historian Nolie Mumey recalled that Fannie Gallagher "wanted to give . . . [Martha] a home and train her to become a member of the family," but that the girl "did not like the discipline. One day Mrs. Gallagher gave her a thrashing, and she objected so strenuously that a miner's committee investigated the incident. As a consequence Mrs. Gallagher refused to have any more to do with her." An article in the *Uinta Chieftain* several years later reported:

But the spirit of original sin itself possessed the girl, and before they had been in their new home six months, the whole camp rang with the depraved [escapades] of Jennie [Martha], the only name she ever known. Young as she was she took to depravity naturally. At last an outrageous offence moved the good old Mrs. Gallagher to inflict a vigorous thrashing. Jennie raised a howl of brutal treatment, and a miners' committee investigated and came to the conclusion that if the girl was thrashed every day it wouldn't improve matters. Mrs. Gallagher now refused to have anything more to do with her, and the miners

raised money to send her to the railroad. This was done, and Jennie
soon made a name for herself along the line of the Union Pacific.

With her brief stay at Fort Bridger and South Pass City reaching their predictable conclusions over a failed meeting of the minds, the miners placed Martha on a stagecoach headed for nearby Piedmont. There, the youngster remained relatively inconspicuous, wandering from one house to another in search of menial employment and odd jobs to keep the wolf from the door.

One area local, Charles Andrews, recalled that fifteen-year-old Martha had been his babysitter during the time his mother ran a boarding house in town. Andrews said that Martha had also helped around the house for a few years until her taste for "social life worried my mother." Andrews recalled that Martha spent most evenings dancing with the soldiers. One day, a neighbor told Ms. Andrews that Martha had been seen dressed in a soldier's uniform at a party she had attended the night before. The implications of exactly how the young girl had come about acquiring a full military uniform were *scandalous* and rocked the town.

"Mother," Andrews went on to say, "blew up and fired her!"

On her own once again, Martha went to work doing odd jobs for the Union Pacific Railroad, including laying track—a brutal, hard, sweaty job usually reserved for only the toughest of men. But the physical work, combined with the social settings of Piedmont, fit with Martha's newly developing view of Calamity Jane's evolving lifestyle. She was forming what for her would become two lifelong tendencies: toughness and spirit. She displayed an open fondness for a male-dominated existence, with its brash and unsettling behavior and erratic activities. These signs plus other symbols of Martha's later life bloomed comfortably in an isolated frontier setting—like microbes in a petri dish—as she grew through her teenage years. Already, she was becoming increasingly comfortable with her Bohemian way of life and more than a little set in her ways.

Fortunately for her, she chose the right community for her "coming out" party.

Piedmont in the late 1860s was a wide-open *Hell on Wheels* kind of town that sprang up along the Union Pacific line. The U.P. was the first of the transcontinental roads to snake its way across Wyoming in 1868/69. Located only eighteen miles west and south of Fort Bridger, Piedmont was at first a rural stagecoach station; but once the railroad began laying track, the town soon enough developed into a water-and-wood refueling stop for trains preparing to face the dauntingly steep climb up the slopes of the Wasatch Range to the west.

Beginning as a tent city in the mid-1860s, Piedmont swelled with homes, like a mushroom patch on a damp hillside. They were occupied by hunters, railroad workers, day laborers, and the members of several large Mormon farm-and-ranch families.

Not surprisingly, the place that Martha called "home" after leaving the Andrews family was composed of seventy-seven male occupants, mostly single laborers, plus sixteen women—nine married and six members of families. Only one—"Martha Cannary," as the census of 1870 revealed—was an unmarried woman with no immediate family ties.

Finding herself alone and not yet grown into adulthood, Martha was a western Americana waif with nothing to rely upon beyond her own wily guiles and the kindness of strangers. With little education and no special training, she wandered around Piedmont looking for various jobs to keep her alive. In the process, she stumbled upon a man hiring laborers for the U.P.—mostly laying track, hauling ties, hammering spikes, and other odd jobs. Martha, standing nearly six feet tall and dressed in buckskins with a wide-brimmed hat on her head and a Bowie knife stuck inside her belt, looked the perfect candidate, according to Don Bacue's *A Dramatization of a Life Called Calamity.*

"You're willing to work hard twelve hours a day?" the man asked her when the line of applicants brought her to his attention. "We can't use any man who won't commit to that." He looked at her hands, calloused and hard, and at her shoulders, wide and straight.

She hoisted one well-worn boot up on the empty chair across the table from him and replied, "Hard work is my middle name," and spat in the general vicinity of a spittoon at the end of the bar.

"Good. You start tomorrow at six as a gandy dancer. Be up at the River Road crossing and report to the foreman. He'll show you what to do."

He signed her and a dozen others up on the spot, never realizing the Union Pacific had just hired the first woman railroader in its history.

After nearly a month of hard work, Martha asked when she could expect to be paid. Her supervisor, a rough, tall, toothy Irishman named Con Shaughnessy originally from County Cork of the Old Sod, laughed, telling her to be patient. "What would you do with money after a week's worth of hard work on the line but lose it in a card game or chasing after some sloe-eyed whore. Another week or so and you'll have your money from the main office. Then you can go to town and tie on a dandy!"

But when another week had passed and the men still hadn't seen their pay, their dispositions took a marked turn for the worse. Finally, on one bright May morning in 1869, a steam engine came chugging onto the horizon several miles southeast of town. By that time, Jane had been promoted to work as a bridge hog, building heavy timber trestles over deep gorges and deeper canyons. As the workers stopped to watch the train's approach, one of them called out: "You know who's on board that there cripple?"

One of the men stood upright, searched the plume of white smoke breaking the cool morning air with his one good eye, and laughed. "About twenty of the prettiest whores this side of Kansas City, I'm hopin'!"

"Better 'n that," the thin man with wiry arms replied.

"They ain't *nothin'* better 'n that," he laughed.

"It's none other than Thomas Clark Durant, the vice president of this here entire Union Pacific line."

Jane looked puzzled. "What in God's hell would a vice president of anything anywhere be doin' this far astray from a civilized town?"

"They're headin' to northern Utah for the payoff. They got a bunch of muckety-mucks onboard goin' to Promontory Summit to celebrate the completion of the transcontinental line. Gonna hold a big *callathump*, some says."

"Git out!" Jane said, spitting, her eyes glued to the growing plume on the horizon. "That's a plain hog-ass lie. Ain't no Promontory Summit in northern Utah. I lived in Utah fer a good spell, and I kin tell you that much from personal experience."

"I'm tellin' you, that's where they're headed. They got a fancy car full o' ex-eck-*kew*-tives along fer the celebration. Ridin' in a car what was built for President Abraham Lincoln hisself afore he was kilt!"

"They're ridin' in a luxury car such as that when we ain't been paid for a week full of Sundays?" The man spat off the side of the bridge they had recently completed constructing. "Now don't that take all?"

"That don't hardly seem right!" someone cried.

Suddenly the supervisor came up to the group and ordered them back to work.

"*You* got paid, then, I reckon," the thin man said, glaring up at Shaughnessy.

"You go on and never mind. All of you. You'll git paid in time." He paused, looking out over the growing number of heads gathering around. "Least so long as you git back to work while you still have a job to git back to!"

Before Martha realized what was happening, the thin man lashed out with a fist that caught the supervisor squarely on the jaw, sending him tumbling backwards, falling into the crowd gathering around to see what was happening.

"Lynch 'im up!" someone called.

"Throw him into the gully!" the one-eyed man said, and as several others pushed him to the edge and rolled him over the side, Con Shaughnessy went tumbling head over heels down the rocky slope nearly thirty feet to the bottom, where he came to an ignominious stop.

"He's dead."

"You kilt 'im."

Martha watched, her heart throbbing, as she saw him slowly raise his head. "No!" she cried. "He just got the wind knocked out of 'im. See? He's movin' some!"

They watched as the man slowly pulled himself to an upright position, shaking the cobwebs from between his ears.

"I say, no money, no bridge crossing!" the one-eyed man called.

"No money, no crossing!" the crowd clanged, and when the one-eyed man gave the orders, the workers began hauling ties from the roadside and stacking them six-high across the rails. When the engineer in the

Victory Train came to within eyeshot of the bridge, he saw the barricade and slammed on the brakes as the mob, waving their tools and crying out for justice, rushed the engine. Several others raced to the back of the train and stormed the VIP car. As several of the workers pulled pistols from their belts and began shooting into the air, Martha caught sight of movement off to the side.

"Con!" she whispered. She stared in horror as the supervisor slowly climbed his way back up the ravine. "Con!" she called, waving him back. She looked around before racing over to him. "What are you doing?"

"I'm gonna stop 'em," he said, pulling an ancient Civil War revolver from his belt. "I'm gonna show 'em they can't push Conway James Shaughnessy around like that and git away with it."

"Con, if you ain't the dumbest . . ." She cut herself short. "Listen, if you ever wanna see County Cork again aside from your dreams, you'll turn around and climb right back down this here gully and follow the draw on back to town."

"I don't wanna see County Cork. I wanna see the dumb-ass little son-of-a-bitch what cold-cocked me face-down on the ground with a .45-caliber hole in his head!"

"Listen to me," she said, her face filled with confusion. "I'm the only friend you got here. You try something like that, they'll kill you fer sure!"

He stopped, paused, taking in the site as the workers crawled over the locomotive's cowcatcher, boiler, and tender like ants over a butter-frosted cake at picnic time. He turned to her.

"I never shoulda let a woman work this crew. I shoulda turned you in the day I found out."

"The day you found out was one of the happiest days of your life, seems I 'call."

He breathed in, looked into her eyes, and sighed. He looked at her, the confusion scarring his face, until she wasn't sure he comprehended what she'd said at all.

"You ever wanna have another day like that, you go on and git afore they kill you fer sure." She reached out. "Gimme that there pea shooter," she said, grabbing the gun from his hand. "And git on down there and back into town!"

As the man turned around and began sidestepping his way back down the slope to the safety of the draw, Martha called after him, "And fer God's sake, stay outa sight!" She watched him safely off before turning and hurrying back to where the mob had stormed the cab and taken the engineer and the fireman hostage, holding them at gunpoint. After several more minutes, Durant, fighting back the only way he could, fired off a telegram to Union Pacific headquarters back East, demanding the immediate wire of funds to the local Western Union Office, which U.P. officials did. The railroad moguls and engineer were released to continue on to the festivities at Promontory Point where they eventually carved their names in history with the driving of the Golden Spike.

Following the Insurrection at Piedmont, the workers cleaned up the site and slipped back into town to spend their money and await the remainder of their pay. Everyone except for Martha Jane. With the excitement of the railroad passing her by, she grew increasingly restless for more action. A census taken in 1870 showed her name missing from Uinta County records. She had left town for good to explore the continuing rumors of precious ore in the small communities throughout the West—strikes that had lured thousands of people to areas such as South Pass City, Atlantic City, and Miner's Delight. Martha was by then "street smart" enough to realize that with rich strikes come easy pickings. And with easy pickings come golden opportunities. She had learned how to drink and carouse while part of the U.P. crew. In town, she accessed the finer points of gambling and flirting with men and shooting to raise holy hell without getting arrested. For the future Calamity Jane, the world was looking good.

And yet, she failed to take advantage of her budding notoriety, laying low until 1874, when she turned up for work at the Kime Store and Boarding House in Miner's Delight, Wyoming. That in itself wasn't particularly memorable, but a local rancher by the name of Tobias (Tobe) Borner, who was destined to become Martha's nephew, detailed something that was.

Johnnie Borner [Tobe's father], as he was known at that time, was running a four-horse team and wagon between Salt Lake and the mines. He would load with clothing and groceries at Salt Lake and sell, or peddle [on] the way to the mines, taking back to Salt Lake, a load of coal on his return trip. Coal was in good demand there. It was on one of these trips to the mines that father was badly hurt, having a broken leg. He was taken to the rooming house where Martha was working.

Martha hadn't yet become widely known for her nursing skills, although she'd had several experiences in treating gunshot wounds, removing arrows, and doctoring illnesses common to the area. Then, in 1878, an outbreak of smallpox flooded Deadwood and, as was the practice at the time, the sheriff and his deputies set up a "pest house" in a remote log cabin in order to isolate the victims of the disease from the town and its petrified residents. Apart from a rare visit from the doctor, the dozen or so stricken patients were left to fend for themselves, presumably to die or, in the best-case scenario, survive the fever only to be left permanently disfigured.

Upon making his first visit to the afflicted, Doctor Babcock, the local physician, did what he could for the stricken before returning to Deadwood to grab something to eat and then stopping by No. 10 Saloon to solicit help to return with him to the cabin. When he found no takers, he returned to the makeshift hospital alone, only to find Martha Jane there, hard at work. Shocked, he asked her if she knew what she was doing. Psychohistory provides us the details:

"I'm ministerin' to the sick and dyin'," she snapped. "What've *you* been doin'?"

The doctor looked at her through saucer eyes. "This man here should by all rights be dead," he said. "He had a fever of a hundred and eight just this morning."

The man rolled his head to look at the Doc and smiled.

"Yeah, well, he ain't a-dyin' on my watch," she said, gritting her teeth as she placed a damp cloth across his brow and filled a spoon with medicine, which she prodded him to swallow.

"Here, now, what's that you're giving him?"

"Jes' sulfur and molasses with a touch o' the jug. It's the only thing I got."

give 'er a chance to heal up good and proper. That means I can't make no more runs from here to Salt Lake. Not for some while."

"Goes without sayin'," she said. "An' that could take months."

He sighed. "That's what worries me. You got a business you can't run for a couple months, surer than Jehova someone else is gonna come along and pick your bones clean. Next thing you know . . ." He shrugged. "No more business."

"Ain't you got no other driver asides yourself?"

"Look around," he said. "Tell me if you see someone standin' in the corner looks like another driver. I got one part-time hired hand out at the ranch, and he's too set in his ways to go wandering around the countryside. He's the only help I got, but he's just plain not able to handle driving a team through Indian Territory. I thought about askin' him, but it just wouldn't be right."

"What would you pay him?"

"What would I pay who?"

"I mean, a driver. If you could find one."

"You know someone? I'll give him going wages and provisions and three percent of the profit on his return."

She thought for several moments.

"You know someone?" he asked again, his brows rising to match his spirits.

"I just might take you up on that."

"You might take me up on what?" He paused. "You mean *you* want to drive the team to Salt Lake?"

"I'm a fair driver. And the price appears right."

He thought some more, squirmed in his chair, and shifted his eyes upward to catch hers. She was smiling.

"Now, wait a minute. I said I'd pay a *man* top wages."

"I heard."

"You're not a man."

She stuffed the last of some gauze and some tape into a satchel she had borrowed from Madam DuFran's brothel down the street, pulled out a flask, and drained half the bottle before handing it to her patient. She bent so near that he could feel the warmth of her breath on his forehead. "I'm glad you noticed," she said. "Not many does."

He shook his head. "I don't know. Don't seem right." He paused, following up with his thought. "You got experience teamin'? Ain't something you just learn how to do overnight, you know."

She stood back upright, put her thumbs inside her belt, and raised one foot up onto the edge of the bed. "Come all the way from Missouri to Salt Lake, and here I am afore you." She opened her eyes wide. "Drove most o' the way myself," she lied.

He rubbed his chin with his right hand. "You sure you can do it?"

"Top wages, provisions, and three percent." She paused. "Man nor woman, no difference to me. You can't git no better 'n that!"

Borner paused, deep in thought.

"*And*," Martha added, winking, "I'll throw in my doctorin' fees for nothin'!"

That clinched the deal. Martha got the job, and Borner got a friend and, as it would turn out, a future sister-in-law in the throes of a strong relationship destined to grow stronger over the next several years. As Borner's son, Tobias, confirmed a decade later:

> *After making his business known and getting acquainted with Miss Canarie [sic], she asked to take the team and make a trip for him to Salt Lake, taking in a load of coal and bringing back a load of goods for the store at South Pass. She made the trip with little or no trouble and brought back a load of food for the camp. Johnnie Borner, not being able to use his leg, let Martha make a second trip. The two trips took about six weeks. By this time winter was coming on and Borner was able to take the outfit back. Martha visited with her brother and sister while in Salt Lake.*

Thus it was that, somewhere in the South Pass / Miner's Delight area of the Wyoming mining camps, the Borners and the Cannarys had met and changed one another's lives forever.

In the meantime, John Borner continued his freighting business after he healed from his broken leg. And Tobias went on with his story:

After delivering to Kime's store, he [Borner] made another trip to Salt Lake with freight for Fort Washakie [previously Camp Brown] and this time he located a ranch of 160 acres, a squatter's right in what is now the Borner's Garden district about four miles above Lander on the Sinks road. This ranch was located in 1874. At that time land was not surveyed, but a man's fence was respected as his land lines. That fall and winter Borner built a two-room log cabin and fenced about 80 acres with a three-pole buck fence.

Borner and a man by the name of Ernest Hornecker, who had come to the valley from Missouri with his stepbrother, John Martin, farmed that land together in 1872, raising grain and potatoes on the running prairie near Sinks Canyon Road, later known as Borner's Garden. Hornecker had written that there were only seven people in the valley in 1872, six men and one woman.

The paucity of settlers was due mostly to the presence of marauding Indians. They had not taken kindly to white miners infringing upon their traditional hunting grounds and grew to be such a menace that, when Hornecker built his house of cottonwood logs in 1872, he cut several "loopholes" in the walls for the placement of guns. Although the Shoshone were friendly, the Sioux were anything but, posing a continuing threat until the Great Sioux War of 1876/77. The men, recognizing the danger, carried guns with them whenever they went about. Often, that wasn't enough.

On July 24, 1873, Mrs. Hattie Hall and Mrs. L. S. Richardson had bid their husbands good-bye at their homes on the Popo Agie River. A band of renegade Indians watched from the nearby hills as the men left their valley homes for the encircling mountains in search of timber. Once they were gone, the warriors swarmed down upon the women, killing and mutilating them—cutting off their appendages and taking their scalps. They plundered their homes, riding off with money and jewelry and killing several head of cattle in the process.

John Borner was initially feared to have been killed too, but he had been fishing on Squaw Creek that day and eventually returned, unaware of what had happened in his absence—but safe.

In the summer of 1875, before making a trip to Salt Lake for the Indian agency, Borner stopped off to see James I. Patten at Camp Brown (later called Fort Washakie). Patten, whose work often kept him away from home for days at a time, told him, "If you can find a woman in Salt Lake that wants to come to the fort, bring her out. I will give her work here and pay her good wages. My wife gets terribly lonesome here."

Martha, who by then had been wandering around the hills and valleys of Wyoming and Montana for nearly a decade, had nevertheless managed to keep in touch with her siblings and knew where to reach them. When Borner ran across Martha at South Pass not long after, he relayed to her what Patten had said.

"Johnnie, are you serious?" she asked.

"His exact words," he said, squinting. "*Why?*"

"Because my sister's been a-stayin' in Salt Lake City, and she's been hankering to come out here! She's stayin' right there in the city with some o' them Mormon polygs. My brother, Lige, too."

Borner's eyes grew wide. "How old?"

"I reckon Lena's just a couple three years younger than me, and Lige a little younger than that. She'd be a *great* companion for Patten's wife. Smart, strong, a hard worker. She's honest. And attractive too. She'd get along really tops with Mrs. Patten. I *know* she would."

He hefted his shoulders. "I don't know. I mean, I think Patten might be looking for someone closer to his wife's own age."

"You bring out Lena and Lige here from the City," she said, "and leave the rest to me. You can take Lena out to the fort to work for the Pattens and Lige can stay with me right here in town."

Borner thought for several seconds before extending his hand.

On his very next trip to Salt Lake City, Johnnie located Lige and Lena—he called her Jennie—exactly where Martha had said he'd find them. He removed them from their foster families and brought them back with him to South Pass City, where they visited with their sister for several weeks before Borner took Lena on to Camp Brown to work for Mrs. Patten. When he saw what a healthy, strapping boy Lige was, he took him on as a hand at his own ranch.

At Camp Brown, Lena adapted well to military life. The camp had been built as an outpost of Fort Bridger, which lay a couple hundred miles to the southwest. Fort Bridger had been named after famed western scout Jim Bridger, who was renowned as one of the first white men to use the Indian trail over South Pass. Legend held that he was the first to taste the waters of the Great Salt Lake, first to report a two-ocean stream, foremost in describing the Yellowstone Park phenomena, and the *only* man to run the Big Horn River rapids on a raft. He also selected the Crow Creek–Sherman Dale Creek route through the Laramie Mountains and Bridger's Pass over the Continental Divide, routes that were eventually adopted by the Union Pacific Railroad.

Unfortunately, he was also a first-class troublemaker, an opportunist, and a thief, but those facts have long since been washed over by the waves of history. So, when gold was discovered near South Pass City, an influx of miners looking to strike it rich flooded the basin. With the Indians a remaining threat to safety in the region, the new outpost was charged with protecting the miners from attacks. In 1878 the post was renamed in honor of Chief Washakie. The chief's daughter had married a white scout. His name: Jim Bridger. Chief Washakie had remained the army's strongest ally against the warring Sioux for years. He lived at the fort under military protection.

Martha periodically visited the fort to see her sister, so the two women often crossed paths with Borner and Chief Washakie. They were a disparate-looking foursome. Lena was of medium build, feminine, and attractive. Martha was nearly six feet tall, full-cheeked, and attired in buckskins. Washakie was leather-faced with broad features chiseled from granite. Borner was smaller than average, standing a little over five feet tall and weighing a scant 135 pounds. His hair was brownish-red, and he had dark blue eyes, sunken yet sharp, was intelligent, and impressing one as being a bit mischievous but shrewd. Everyone who met him liked him, including Martha.

Born in Saxony, Germany, Borner had emigrated to Wisconsin as a child, working on the family farm until the Civil War broke out. He enlisted in the Union Army on September 25, 1861, in Company A,

Twelfth Wisconsin Infantry. After serving for only seven months, he was admitted to the hospital with chronic hepatitis and severe diarrhea—common wartime afflictions. He was discharged due to his disability on December 20, 1862. When he was finally healed three years later, he reenlisted in the Fiftieth Wisconsin, organized at Camp Randall in Madison. He served until the conclusion of the war, when he was mustered out a little more than a year later.

After leaving the service, Borner worked on a Union Pacific construction crew, living in Salt Lake City for two years. After that, he joined the gold rush to Wyoming, settling in an area four miles north of Lander that eventually became known as Borner's Gardens.

Once Borner had gotten Lena settled in at Fort Washakie and Lige put up in his new job, he was able to take life a little easier. The boy at the time was living in South Pass with Martha outside of Lander. His relationship with Borner seemed solid from the start—"forged from steel," as Borner later termed it.

Martha, too, felt the burden of responsibility suddenly lifted from her shoulders. With Lena safe and secure in the care of the Pattens, Martha got the urge to move on once more. The time was right to begin laying plans for her next great adventure. This time, she set her sights on the Black Hills of Dakota Territory to satisfy her needs.

This time, too, for the first time ever, she seriously considered bringing along a traveling companion. She settled on her baby brother, Lige.

CHAPTER FIVE

A Rude Awakening

Martha Jane was nothing if not purposeful and predictable. She was her own worst enemy, her own best friend. She was the only Calamity Jane she knew, the one she created, the one she promoted, the one she believed. These are her words.
    —DON BACUE, *A DRAMATIZATION OF A LIFE CALLED CALAMITY*

IN RESEARCHING THE LIFE AND TIMES OF CALAMITY JANE, AUTHOR, editor, and scriptwriter Don Bacue took into consideration a number of documented descriptions and traits and ran them through a psychohistorical lens, analyzing the genealogical influences of Martha Jane from afar, deducing her life, her goals, her actions, her words—what the real Martha Jane Cannary may likely have said, thought, and done at any given period in her life. Writing about a time from which precious little documentation exists, Bacue analyzed the relationship of Martha Jane—before she morphed into Calamity—to her family, particularly her brother, Elijah.

❦

FROM ACT ONE
Martha Jane and Lige left South Pass City on horseback, headed for Fort Laramie, where the Jenney Expedition was assembling to begin its assault on the Black Hills of South Dakota. The trip to the fort was slotted to take four or five days, depending upon conditions.

"Remember," Martha told her brother in preparation for the trip ahead. "If anything can go wrong, it will."

"I'm not scared."

"That's what worries me."

"*Aww!*"

"A person travelin' all alone kin get sick, fall off his horse, and die."

"Have to be a pretty *dumb* person."

"Or," she said, ignoring his sarcasm, "his horse kin get ill and stumble along until it can't hardly travel no more, exposin' the rider to all sorts o' bad elements. Or it kin stumble and break its leg or lame-up and have to be shot or abandoned, leaving the rider all alone to travel the rest of the way on foot."

"That wouldn't bother me. I'm a good walker."

"Not with a dozen mounted Sioux warriors on your ass, you ain't."

"You're jes' worryin' fer nothin'."

"Or," she continued, intent upon impressing a sense of caution in the boy, "a rider kin wash off the saddle while crossin' a stream and drown. Dang near had that happen to me once."

"Really?"

"Or, worse yet, he kin go tumbling into the river and bouncing off the boulders all the way downstream till he washes up onshore, good as dead and ready for the vultures to start peckin' at his eyes. Or he kin lose his rations and starve to death or lose his water and die from thirst. He kin be attacked by wild animals and kilt, or he could be ravaged by savage Indians to the worst outcome imaginable." She paused to look at him. "That's what kin happen to a rider all alone out here in the wilderness."

"Well, we ain't all alone. We got each other."

Martha knew all too well that argument was coming. She understood that, with Lige at her side, she might have felt more comfortable, but she didn't. She realized that, for two people on a cross-country journey spanning several days, the trip wasn't twice as safe, it was two times twice as dangerous.

"That's even worst—two people travelin' together."

He looked up at her. "Whaddya mean?"

"With two people crossing the country, they make fer twice the targets for savage Indians. Or twice the chance of one of their horses stumbling and having to be put down, and the rider would have to double up, exceptin' the additional weight on that horse kin take its toll and that horse have to be put down, too." She paused, searched his face, his eyes never straying far from the trail ahead. "Or, two people mean twice the food you gotta have, twice the water, and twice the chance for accidents to befall 'em—and twice the chance for sickness. With one person down with the ills, the other would have to remain behind to care for 'im—if only it turned out for the best for everyone, which ain't 'xactly no foregone conclusion."

"What's that mean, 'foregone conclusion'?"

"Means, ain't necessary fer sure."

"Oh."

"And remember that two riders also means twice the necessity fer cover and twice the ammunition and twice the will to carry on. If one grows tired of the journey, what would the other one do but leave him behind, making his own risks that much greater, not to mention them of his partner."

So, either way you slice it, Martha said, the journey to Fort Laramie was not without its perils. And one of the most worrisome of all for her was turning out to be Lige, himself.

—⁓—

Three days had passed, and they had made good time when, on the morning of the fourth day, Martha spied Lige from the corner of her eye as he edged his horse off the trail and into the tall grass.

"What are you doin'?"

"A mulie buck," he said curtly, reaching for his rifle.

She scanned the horizon. "Mulie buck, my ass. There's nothin' out there but trouble. Let's keep moving."

Suddenly she saw the boy whip his spurs into the horse's haunches and take off in a gallop, shrieking like a wild Indian as he bolted away.

"Lige!" she called after him, her words falling on the stubborn prairie breeze.

"*Whee-oop! Whee-whee-whee! Whee-oop!*" he yelled, and within moments, he was gone from sight.

Several hours later, Martha found herself settled into an open meadow backed up to a thick grove of aspens. She had begun making camp for the evening when she heard a horse approaching through the thicket. She instinctively drew her pistol, relieved at last to see the approaching rider was Lige.

"What the hell is the matter with you, riding off like that? And after I so recent told you 'bout the dangers of reckless behavior on the prairie. Where are you brains?"

After chastising him for having ridden off that way—risking his life as well as hers—the two settled down, Lige poking at the fire, as Martha heated a pot of coffee to boiling. Dining on hardtack and elk jerky, washed down with the steaming brew made from water they'd gotten from a small spring just uphill, they finished eating and began cleaning up as well as they could in order to get an early start in the morning. Stuffing their plates and cups back into their bags, Martha threw another small log on the fire as the two settled in for the night.

Lige, looking up into the black moonless sky, turned to his sister. "Marthy?"

She paused. "I'm the only one here, damn it to hell."

He squinted at her. "Why?"

"Why? Whatcha mean, *why*?"

"You know. Why are you here?" He waited but got no response. "Why are *we* here? I mean, what are we doing here?"

She sighed. "You got a reason for askin' such a dumb-ass question or what? You know Goddamn well why we're here. We're gonna get to the fort afore them back-East assholes leaves on that expedition to the Black Hills and winds up with all the gold."

"No, I mean . . . I mean, I'm just wonderin' . . . I know why we're *here*. But is that all there is for you? Bein' somewhere where you wasn't at yesterday? Is it just because you want to have another adventure? Is it 'cuz you wanna see somethin' new? Or is it some other reason?" He paused, adding apologetically. "I mean, I'm only askin' because I'm just wonderin'."

Martha suppressed a smile. "Aren't you a might young to be askin' such deep-thinkin' questions as them?"

"I'm serious," he said. "You don't seem like you know why you do half the things you do sometimes, and I'm wonderin' if it's a man you're lookin' fer, someone to get married to and settled in, and that's why. Or is it just travelin' around the country gittin' time and experiences under your belt. Or is it the thrill of the new towns and the new people or what."

Martha thought for several moments, the smile on her face beginning to fade.

"I guess I never really thought about it a whole lot afore. Though now that you mention it, 'taint no man I'm hankerin' fer. I know *that* fer sure."

"How come?"

"Men are all alike. Present company 'scluded," she said leaning in toward the boy and tipping her hat.

He smiled. "Don't seem hardly right. Near's every woman I ever knew was looking' to git hitched, settled in, have a couple dozen screamin' kids and a proper name carved into her front door and . . . oh, hell, just havin' a front door *period!*"

She jumped up. "A couple *dozen*?!"

"Come on, you know what I mean." His eyes twinkled by the campfire. "You too old so soon to start havin' kids?"

She shook her head. "Sometimes you say the God-damnedest things."

"Well?"

"Well . . ." she said, throwing it back on the boy. "What about *you*? What is it *you're* a-wantin' outa life? Nobody forced *you* to come along." She paused, leaning in toward him once more. "You can ride, you can ranch, you can shoot straight, you got a good head on your shoulders." She hesitated. "*Most* of the times!" She pulled back, took a stick, and poked the fire until the flames reignited. "Least you're not like this old doorknob atop my own fool neck. And don't tell me it ain't one of them fancy nice-smellin' ladies I know you had yore eye on fer most of your growed-up life. Livin' in the Great Salt Lake and all. Probably one o' them Mormon gals, tall and slender and cuddly-uppity. That'd be just like you. That'd be just like the kind o' gal you'd cotton up to."

His hand shot out and poked her in the side. "No such thing!"

"No such thing," she taunted, lowering her head and spitting on the ground that separated them. "Yeah, right. Like you git a chance, you're gonna turn 'em away. Beat 'em back with a stick. That's you, all right. That's ol' love-em-and-leave-em Lige."

"I didn't say I'd turn none back, necessary. It's just that I'm thinking maybe someday I'll meet someone . . . you know, nice. Like mom and all. But until then, I figure a fella should have at least as much high-country spirited adventure as his very own sister. I'm just wonderin' if that's what life is all about fer you."

"I couldn't tell you half the high-country adventures I already had, even if I was to try. You end up owning up to half of 'em at the end of your lifetime, and you'll have somethin' to hang your hat on. I Goddamn guarantee."

Martha turned back to the fire, pulled her hat a little lower down onto her forehead, and settled back against her saddle, thrown up against a large limestone rock outcropping turtling its head out of the grass like a prairie dog. Several moments passed before she heard her brother's voice once more.

"What was she like?"

Martha stopped, her brows furrowed. "*What?* . . . What was *who* like?"

"Maw. You know. What was she *really* like. Died so young I can't hardly remember nothin' 'bout her 't all. Not really. Not as a fact."

Martha breathed in, holding her breath for several moments before expelling the air far louder than she'd intended.

"Not much to remember, I reckon."

"You must remember more than me. I was still a baby. You wuz, what, ten, twelve year old by then?"

Martha paused. "Reckon' closer to fourteen."

"Fourteen. So you musta know'd her pretty well." His voice shared a hint of excitement as the crickets grew steadily louder behind them. "I mean, you wuz with her a good part o' your life."

"Reckon'."

"Was she a good God-fearin' woman? I guess . . . I mean, she loved the Lord and honored the Sabbath and could quote from the good book and all. Like the Mormons used to do when I was with 'em. Ever' night, practical, we'd have to get down on our knees and say our blessin's to Jehovah."

"That's a lot of prayin'," Martha grinned. "Ever' night."

"Now, I'm serious. Is that the way our maw was, too? Prayerful toward the Lord and all?"

"*I don't know!*" Martha snapped, catching her breath and expelling it sharply. "What I mean is, I don't know what was in her heart and what wasn't. Always seemed fearful of the Lord. A powerful God-loving woman. Always sticking up fer her children, always protective. I guess she was a good God-fearing Christian lady, all right. I guess you could say that much 'bout her."

"I thought so. I mean, I just know'd our mom would be a decent Christian woman and all."

Martha paused. "Yeah."

After several more moments, Lige continued. "What wuz we back then? We wuz maw and paw and you and Lena, right? Lena was there, too, right?"

"Yes," Martha said. "Lena was there, too. And young Cilus. He was just a baby. Used to call out, 'Som-bitch,' 'cause he couldn't say all the words straight out."

"Oh, yeah. My older brother. He died young."

Martha thought for several moments, her eyelids growing steadily heavier. "Yeah, he died young."

"But he remembered maw, too. Cilus, I mean. He must have remembered her, too. Bein' born so much afore me and all. He had to have remembered her, too."

Martha felt herself nodding her head. "Yes," she whispered. "He remembered her, too." And she thought back. She thought back to a time months before. Years before. A lifetime before. Or at least so it seemed to her. A time before Lige was even born.

- ⚬ -

From ACT TWO

"You *som*-bitch!"

Martha Jane looked down and laughed. She watched as Cilus threw himself against the straw stacked nearly to the sky, scrambling with his five-year-old frame, his young limber body all arms and legs clawing against the dried dusty pile as he struggled to mount the summit.

"Yore a daisy if you think!" Martha chided, laughing at her younger brother's feeble efforts. "Sides, Paw'll tan yore britches he catches you cussin' like that."

"Yeah! Ain't like yore so pure!"

She reached down. "Give me yore hand," she said.

"So you can shove me off agin? Don't think so this time!"

"Come on. No tricks. Cross my heart." She made a quick sign of the cross before extending her palm as he got a foothold in the pile and held himself firm, slapping her hand away. The suddenness pitched her off balance and sent her tumbling backwards onto her ass. The straw dust rose in a plume like the cannon fire at Gettysburg, finally settling on her like miniature snowflakes over the Missouri prairie. Recognizing his opportunity, Cilus scrambled with all his might for the pinnacle.

"You little son-of-a-bitch!" she cried, dusting herself off. "You cheatin' little smart ass!" She struggled to stand upright again. "No fair, you little asshole!"

"*You're* the asshole!" he called, laughing, clawing his way nearly to the top. He lunged forward suddenly, grabbing her ankle, her dress flying out to the sides, her hands flailing at the straw in a feeble attempt to regain control. Suddenly she felt herself sliding down the side of the mountain, grasping for her brother. When she hit the ground, she looked up at him as he grinned down triumphantly.

"No fair!" she called again, adding under her breath, "Filthy little bugger." She looked up again. "You cheated!"

He laughed.

"It's not funny. I'll git yore skinny ass now!" She scrambled around to the back of the pile to attempt another assault. "I'll show *you* who the son-of-a-bitch is!"

She looked up into her brother's face, suddenly turned to granite.

"Oh, oh," he said.

She turned and scanned the barnyard to where her gaze fell short upon a solitary figure. She froze.

"Martha Jane!"

She hesitated for only a moment. "Yeah, Paw?"

"You and your filthy mouth get your ass over here right now!"

"Oh, crap," she muttered as Cilus plopped down and crab-crawled to the edge of the mountain. As he slid down to the ground, Martha walked up to her father, wondering just how long he'd been standing there.

"Yeah, Paw?" she said again. "You want somethin'?" She looked up into his eyes, roiling with anger. His hand shot out suddenly, his big meaty palm catching her squarely across the face. She stumbled back three steps.

"What did I tell you about using such foul language? What have I told you over and over again about that?"

She instinctively reached up to salve her stinging cheek. "You said not to use them words."

"I said not to use them words."

She nodded as he reached out and grabbed her arm so tightly she let out a squeal. Her mother opened the door to the house and stepped out onto the porch. "What's going on out here?"

"Never you mind," Robert said, pulling his daughter up onto the aching wooden planks, past his wife, and into the house. Grabbing a bar of soap, he plopped onto a chair and, pulling her down over his knees, forced the bar into her mouth.

"I'll teach you once and for all to curse like some gutter whore!"

Charlotte came in, her face scarred with fear. "Bob, don't. Please. There's no need for . . ."

"You shut up!" he snapped. "If you'd been a better example for her, I wouldn't have to do this!"

"But . . ."

"But *nothing*," he said, turning back to the young girl on his lap, coughing and struggling to catch her breath. Pulling a cord from around his waist, he doubled it up and slapped it down against her bottom. Hard.

Thwack! Thwack! Thwack!

Martha tried to cry out, but the soap caught in her teeth, muffling her sobs.

Several more cracks, and he pulled her up off his lap and threw her down to the floor. Towering over the sobbing youngster, he strung the rope back through his pants and looked from his daughter to his wife—over to his son, standing in the doorway, an air of horror hanging over his face, not knowing what lay in store for him. Robert looked once again at Martha and ripped the foaming bar from the girl's mouth, tears running down her face. "Get up. Get up!" he glowered. "And if I ever hear you use that kind of language again, I'll give you more of the same, do you hear? You think that was bad, you just do that again and I'll teach you what it means to be whupped within an inch of yore life!"

As the woman went to her daughter's side to help her to her feet, Robert Cannary stomped off toward the door, his son stepping nimbly aside, and stormed out into the daylight and the unsettling heat of a northern Missouri afternoon.

—◦—

"How did it taste?"

She glared at him as he lay on the bed, looking confused and still frightened. She rummaged through some nightclothes on the stand pushed up against the rough-hewn whitewashed wall. "How do you think it tasted, you dumb shit?"

"It must have been *awful*." He shook his head and shuddered. "I got some suds splashed agin' my eyes once and I thought I was gonna go blind."

"It's lye, stupid. That's like an acid or something. Like . . ." She thought for several seconds. "Like orange juice or vinegar. Shit like that."

The boy stopped to think. "You better now?"

Martha Jane opened her mouth and lifted her tongue.

"Holy Christ. Your mouth's all burnt an' *red*!"

She selected a nightgown, slipped behind a dressing screen, and proceeded to change out of her clothes. "Don't hurt none. Not no more."

"It *don't?*"

She disappeared for a second before her head popped back up above the screen like a bobber on a line with a tommy cat at one end. She fastened the buttons on the front of her gown up around her neck. "Nothin' hurts no more." She turned toward him and motioned with her head toward the downstairs. "You wash up fer bed?"

"I washed up before supper," he said, grabbing his shoes and pulling them off before slipping his pants and shirt off, undressing down to his socks and BVDs. He pulled back the comforter and slipped underneath.

She thought for several seconds and sighed. "Lena's tucked in next door. She's sound asleep. I'm gonna turn in, too, I reckon." Lifting the latch on the handle, she opened the door and stopped. "Night, Cy," she said softly.

"Night, Marthy."

———

The sun had disappeared below the horizon hours earlier when Martha found herself stirring. Her eyes popped open to the accompaniment of sounds snaking their way up the cabin stairs. Checking on her younger sister awash in the moonlight, she slipped out from her straw-bale mattress and crept across the floor. Opening the door, she heard more noises and peeked out and down the hall. Cy's door was still shut tight. Thinking for a moment there might be an animal that had gotten into the house—some coons or possums or even a black bear—she took several short, halting steps down the stairs, stopping with each one to listen. And then, just as suddenly as the sounds had started, they stopped. Replaced by giggling. Moaning. *Whispering*. She thought about calling out but decided better of it.

Peeking around the corner, she could barely make out anything in the soft warm light of the fireplace flickering across the floor, the last of the embers casting crazy loon-like shadows upon two figures sitting upright, face-to-face.

"You clean?" one of the figures giggled.

"You care?"

She saw her mother nod her head. "Course I care." She laughed softly. "I don't want no filthy farmer messin' up *my* kitty."

"Oh, yeah," he said, grabbing for her, her mother's bare shoulders hiding his hand from Martha's view. He raised his brows. "Like I'm sure you cared all so hellfire much back at the kitty farm."

She threw her head back, her long copper hair flying in all directions, the orange glow against the runaway strands coaxing them to life.

Martha could see the figures more clearly as they pulled apart from one another. And then her mother bent slowly forward. "How many times do I have to tell you, it wasn't nothin' like that."

"You mean you worked there and never had a man? They just paid you to talk dirty to . . ." He stopped short, grunting as she lowered her head down against his lap. "*Ohh . . . ohhhh . . .*"

She made some strange sounds with her throat, sounds Martha had never heard before. And then her father let out another soft groan, dropping his head back to expose his throat, his bare chest, his weight laid back against his arms, his palms pushing against the soft pinewood floor. After her mother had spent several minutes ministering to him, she sat up. Basking in the glow of the light, her skin crackled with excitement. He grunted.

"I had my druthers," she said, smiling.

"I'll bet you did," he said, pulling her neck to his mouth as she threw her head back, her body straining, her arms tightening around his waist as he maneuvered himself between her thighs, duck-walking in on his knees until he was satisfied he could get no closer.

"Sides, isn't that what attracted your attentions in the first place? My considerable talents with the gents?"

"What attracted me to you in the first place was these fantastic dairies of yours," he said, pulling back from her far enough to grab a breast in each hand and squeeze.

"*Dairies?*" She threw her head back once more and laughed, more loudly this time, loud and steady, unexpectedly wicked, wanton, *possessed.* "Did you say *dairies?*" She laughed several more times.

"*Shh!*" He motioned with his finger.

"Leave it to a farm boy!" she said, more quietly this time.

"Leave *what* to a farm boy?" His breath grew shorter, his voice higher in pitch and louder as he pressed himself against her. "You got something against farm boys all of a sudden? You holdin' out for something better? For one a' them cowboys who come shooting up to you like a buckin' bronco?"

"*Umm,*" she said as his hands moved around her neck, her back, his fingers massaging, manipulating, taunting, teasing. "You gonna break this li'l ol' filly, Bob? That what you mean to do? Break me good once and fer all? So I don't have to go lookin' for it in town no more?"

"What do you do in town?" he asked, his breathing becoming strained.

"You know damn well what I do in town."

He paused, nibbling on her again. "What? Tell me. I want to hear it."

"I tease 'em."

"Tease who?"

"The men."

"How?"

"How do you think?"

"*How?*" he said, his voice growing short.

"With my considerable womanly charms. Once I give 'em a glimpse, they get all excited and wanna come back for more."

"And then what?"

"Why, Robert Wilson Cannary, I do believe you are *jealous*. How quaint!"

"And *then* what?" he reiterated.

"And then what do you think?" she asked, her voice growing strained, her breathing becoming more rapid.

"*And then what?*"

"And then," she said, her words increasingly animated, like the waves on a lake with the winds whipping the water to froth, "I hike up my skirt and let 'em feel up just about anything they want. Just as far as they want."

Robert grabbed her by the calves, his hands working their way slowly up her thighs. "Like this?"

"*Uh-huh.*"

"And then?"

"And then, if they're real good and real strong and real handsome, I give 'em a little feel of what's in store for them before I take them upstairs and give 'em a show in private."

She leaned forward, lowered her head, and grabbed his face suddenly, squeezing her palms against his cheeks like a vice, moving close enough to kiss him. "Is that what you want to hear? Is that what you have in mind for me, too, cowboy?"

"Oh, my God, you make me so all-fired hot. I can't stand the thought of you being with another man. And I can't stand the thought of you *not*."

"Does that turn you on?"

"That . . ." he whispered, "turns . . . me . . . *on!*"

"So? What are you going to do about it?"

"What I'm going to do about it," he said, his voice growing more menacing, gruff, his demeanor changing in an instant, reminding Martha of the wrath she had experienced at the hands of her father earlier in the day, "is to bring you to your knees, begging for mercy."

For a moment Martha thought about turning, leaving, creeping as silently back up the stairs as she had slipped down, up and back behind the safety of her bedroom door, the warmth and security of her covers. She shivered at the thought of what might happen next, terrified of what he might do if he caught her there. And then she heard words she had never heard before.

"What I'm going to do about it is satisfy you like you ain't never been satisfied before. Better, better than *anybody* else *ever* . . . better than any one of 'em has *ever* done you before!"

He paused, nibbling her ear before biting down on it, a sharp yelp escaping from her lips. "Do you until you cry out with joy." And then she began to laugh again, deep and guttural this time—loud, sharp, staccato laughter exploding against the aging logs of the cabin bearing witness to the night. She lay herself down, and Martha caught a quick glimpse between her legs.

Wow, the girl thought. *Maw ain't got nothin' down there but fur, either.* Exactly what some of the neighboring boys had intimated she herself should have had by the time she had turned twelve, that some of the boys teased her about, taunting her, the older ones chiding her for what she *didn't* have down there, *daring* her to prove them wrong. Suddenly it was all clear. Nothing there but a perfectly styled matt of curly red hair that her father was preparing to assault.

Is that *what they'd meant?* she wondered, her pulse quickening as she thought back to the time a local boy had grabbed her in the swimming hole, squeezed her to him, and pretended to try to kiss her, all the while edging his hand between her thighs when one of the other boys warned him to stop. *She ain't even old enough to have nothin' between her legs what'd do you no good anyhows!*

At the time, she thought he'd meant a penis. Like her brother possessed. Now, suddenly, she realized different.

Martha watched her parents in horror—transfixed by the sight, knowing and not knowing what was going to happen next. Could it be? Was this actually about to unfold before her very eyes? Should she leave? Should she stay? *Could* she leave?

Suddenly she felt something brush against her leg and whirled around.

"*Ohh!*" she gasped, catching herself short.

"What is it?" a male voice said. Cy's hand gripped her nightdress, his free hand on her hip as he bent forward to peer past her. "Where's that noise comin' from?"

Martha panicked, guilt breaking her brow. She shoved her finger against her lips. "*Shhh,*" she said. "It's nothing. "Go on back to bed."

"But, what is it? What's happening?"

"Come on," she whispered. "Let's go." And as she took him by the hand and led him quietly back up the stairs, she paused only long enough to hear her mother cry out softly.

"Oh, do me, cowboy. Do me good and hard, like I need to be done. Do me like Dixon does. Do me like ever' time I go to town!"

"What was that?" Cy asked, confused.

"Nothing," Martha said, ushering him back into his room and into bed. "It's just . . . the wind."

And as he climbed back under the covers, he frowned. "Who's *Dixon?*"

Martha Jane paused. "No one," she said softly. "Absolutely no one at all."

──────

FROM **ACT THREE**

Lige rolled over on his side, pushed at one of the logs until it crackled and hissed against the blackness of the night. He cleared his throat. "It's funny, you know?"

Martha looked over at him. "What is?"

"Well, I mean, here we both are. And you knew maw, and Lena did. And Cirus, and he's gone. And o' course, paw. I'm about the only one around who didn't know her a'tall. Least not so's I kin recall."

"Sometimes," Martha said under her breath, "it's better that way."

"You know, my not ever really knowin' our maw and all, sometimes I look at you and I have the strange feeling as if I'm lookin' right at maw, like I'm not with you a'tall but with her. You know? I know it sounds funny, but the things you do, the things you say, the places you've see'd by yourself. Where you been off to. Just like maw. Both of you leavin' the farm for the excitement of prospectin' for gold and all. Both of you comin' out here to the West. I guess what I'm sayin' is, I look at you and I picture our maw. And somehow, picturin' that, seein' a picture of her in my mind, I don't really miss her all that much. Maybe I should, I don't know. But it's almost like when I'm lookin' at you, I'm seein' the spitting image of our maw. Ain't that queer?"

Martha took a deep breath and rolled over. "I don't know. Maybe . . . it ain't so queer."

"You ever git the feelin' maybe there's something more to life than what you already know?"

She paused, picked up a stick, and poked at the fire. "Course I do. Nobody knows ever-thing."

"Well, then, how we 'sposed to find out?"

"Find out what?"

"You know, 'bout life. With Maw gone and Paw gone, who's left to teach us what the answers is? Who's left to tell us?" He paused momentarily. "'Lest you. 'Lest you know all there is to know 'bout life to teach it to me." He paused, his eyes widening. "Do you?"

"No such thing as knowin' all there's to know 'bout life. No matter how old a person gits."

He sighed, apparently completely out of questions, even though he looked far from satisfied. "Yeah. I guess that's prob'ly true."

"Course it is." She yawned. "Got an early start ahead of us tomorrow, we want to make fort by sundown. We'd best get some sleep." She listened to the sound of the leather squawking as her brother pushed his head back up against his saddle.

"Night, Marthy," he said, closing his eyes.

Several moments passed before Martha replied. "Night, Lige."

CHAPTER SIX

The Jenney Expedition and Deadwood

It's easy for a woman to be good who has been brought up with every protection from the evils of the world and with good associates. Martha wasn't that lucky. She was a product of the wild and woolly west. She knew better than anyone where she made her mistakes, and she didn't rate her virtues as highly as her friends did.
                    —DORA DUFRAN, BLACK HILLS, SOUTH DAKOTA,
                              MADAM AND BROTHEL OWNER

KNOWING THAT LENA WAS SAFE IN PATTEN'S CARE, MARTHA DISGUISED herself in soldier's clothes and, along with Lige, joined the Jenney expedition in 1875 to the Black Hills of Dakota Territory. The expedition followed the 1874 Custer trek to the Black Hills, which had been organized to confirm that the gold discovered there was of a large enough quantity to warrant opening the area to white miners. By the time Martha's true identity was discovered, the expedition was too far from the fort to send her back, so she was demoted to teamster and camp cook. After that, she often rode in the wagon with Sam Young, an experienced teamster. Of course, she never mentioned her demotion in her autobiography, in which she stated:

> *Was then ordered to the Black Hills to protect miners, as that country was controlled by the Sioux Indians and the government had to send the soldiers to protect the lives of the miners and settlers in that section. Remained there until fall of 1875 and wintered at Fort Laramie.*

In fact, she wasn't actually there to protect the miners at all but rather to explore the region. Elijah accompanied her to the Black Hills in 1875, as a Chicago newspaper correspondent confirmed in June of that year. "She wanted to see the Hills; so donning a suit of blue, and taking her brother, a lad of 16, whom she supports, with her, she got into a government wagon, and, with the help of drivers and soldiers, here she is."

In an article entitled, "The Gold-Hunters," the subheading read: "Lesser Notables . . . 'California Joe,' 'Tige,' and 'Calamity Jane'—Their Curious Antecedents." From the subheading, it's fairly clear that Lige was the "Tige" referred to in the reference.

By 1875 Martha was already being called Calamity Jane—a moniker she was happy to embrace. A Cheyenne newspaper had verified that a woman who had accompanied the soldiers to the Black Hills went by that very name.

A man named McMillan, who had attended the World's Fair and written of the Black Hills exhibit, accompanied the Jenney expedition, recalling that Calamity was the third white woman in history to visit the Hills. He described her as a "poor thing" and "a veritable daughter of the regiment, who dressed in men's clothes and accompanied the troops nearly six months during their wanderings."

Calamity recorded in her autobiography that she had left the Black Hills in the fall of 1875 and wintered at Fort Laramie. Elijah most likely returned to the Borners' ranch in Sinks Canyon after that. It wasn't long before John Borner's growing infatuation with eighteen-year-old Lena was apparent. When he finally asked her to become his wife, she was thrilled. Borner left Elijah to tend the ranch while he rode off with Lige's sister to Lander City, where they were married on September 23, 1875.

Following their wedding, the thirty-four-year-old groom escorted his new bride to a section of land he owned at the foot of the Sinks Canyon on the Popo Agie River near Lander, Wyoming. Elijah most likely joined them and lived there with them for the coming year.

When Lena bore her husband a child on May 4, 1876, Calamity was too busy to pay her respects to the couple and their newborn, whom they named May Rebecca. Calamity's autobiography hints at a hectic period in her life:

In spring of 1876, we were ordered north with General Crook to join Gen'ls Miles, Terry and Custer at Big Horn river. During this march I swam the Platte river at Fort Fetterman as I was the bearer of important dispatches. I had a ninety mile ride to make, being wet and cold, I contracted a severe illness and was sent back in Gen. Crook's ambulance to Fort Fetterman where I laid in the hospital for fourteen days.

Even though Calamity *did* ride with Crook's command, it's doubtful she was *ordered* to do so. More likely she snuck into the regiment twice—once in February 1876 and again the following June. General Crook did send her back to Fort Fetterman, as Calamity wrote, but it wasn't because she was sick. As soon as Crook discovered that she was a "camp follower," he packed her off to the fort with the wounded.

Not surprisingly, Calamity's autobiography included an adventurous escapade or two along with accounts of the campaign to bring the Sioux and Cheyenne back to their reservations, an exercise in futility that ultimately led to George Custer's disastrous defeat and death at the Battle of the Little Big Horn.

Still, Calamity was nothing if not industrious. In addition to turning favors for Crook's soldiers, she had been observed hanging around several houses of prostitution, known as "hog ranches," along the Cheyenne-Deadwood Trail in 1876. Along that trail lay the Three Mile Road Ranch, aptly named for its positioning a scant three miles above Fort Laramie. Adolph Cuny and Jules Ecoffey established the road ranch as a stage stop in 1873 and soon added a store and other buildings, as well as a sod corral, where they sold hay and grain. They advertised their ranch in the local papers, boasting of its billiard hall, blacksmith shop, and café that served meals at all hours of day or night. Later, as a business perk, they built eight two-room cottages for prostitutes. Calamity was said to have been one of the shady ladies who worked there. She was alleged to have frequented other hog ranches as well.

Documentation of Calamity's presence in the Black Hills as early as 1876 comes in the form of an unimpeachable source. After gold seekers had swarmed the area, Calamity followed them to Custer City in the southern Black Hills, where gold was originally discovered. It's clear that she made Custer City her "home"; in 1876, according to town records, Captain Crawford, a law officer in Custer City at the time, arrested her for "intoxication and disorderly conduct."

The following month, on May 4, Calamity was seen on the trail from Cheyenne leading a party of gold seekers in search of their fortunes. Not long after, toward the end of the month, she was a resident of the Cheyenne jail after being arrested for grand larceny. She had allegedly stolen some women's clothing. But the jury found her not guilty, and before long, she was on the road again, this time journeying east to visit the hog ranches along the route to Fort Laramie.

In her autobiography, Calamity wrote: "When able to ride I started for Fort Laramie where I met Wm. Hickock [Hickok], better known as Wild Bill, and we started for Deadwood, where we arrived about June."

Unfortunately, Calamity's documentation omitted a few illuminating facts. Although she met Wild Bill Hickok on her way to Fort Laramie to enlist enough members to press on to Deadwood over the treacherous Cheyenne-Deadwood Trail, Calamity was in no condition to realize it. During the week that Custer's Battle at the Little Bighorn in Montana unfolded, an officer asked Hickok's party if they would take a young woman along with them in their search for gold. The woman had been drinking with the soldiers and causing trouble and had been quarantined in the stockade for several days. Steve Utter, a member of the party, stepped forward, saying he knew of a woman named Calamity Jane and volunteered to take care of her on their journey. When Utter discovered that she didn't have any suitable clothes and, in fact, was nearly naked, the party members pitched in and gathered together some buckskin clothing that she could wear on the trail.

When in June 1876 Hickok and his party had signed on enough prostitutes, prospectors, gamblers, liquor peddlers, and one "respectable" family seeking a better life, he left for Deadwood and Fort Laramie. Calamity was right with them, along with a five-gallon keg of whiskey that Hickok had brought along for "medicinal purposes." By then, Calamity had become a slave to whiskey and often partook of the contents of Hickok's "golden keg."

White Eye Anderson, who was one of the Hickok party, recalled Calamity as a "big-hearted woman" despite the tall tales she told around the evening campfires. She helped White Eye prepare the meals and pack the grub box when they broke camp in the mornings.

On July 12, after two weeks on the trail, the Hickok party arrived in Deadwood. After settling in, Calamity hung out around the Hickok and Utter camp—possibly for the good camaraderie she found there, but more likely for the even better food. Seeing her so often in the vicinity Hickok may have triggered the rumors of a romance, rumors Calamity never exactly rushed to extinguish. But from day one Anderson didn't buy the story, insisting that Calamity and Hickok had never been more than platonic acquaintances.

How much of this was true and how much fancy? Not everyone could agree. A notorious local prostitute named Madam Dora DuFran had her own take on Calamity's contribution to the Black Hills days.

A long-time friend and occasional employer of Calamity, DuFran no doubt had insights into the legend that most others did not. Still, her accounts have to be taken with a large grain of salt: She never bothered to write down her thoughts until well after Calamity's passing. Regardless, some of what the self-proclaimed "Brothel Madam" had to say is interesting.

—◆—

In the autumn of 1876, after the Custer Massacre, which took place in June, General Crook was ordered to clean up the roving bands of Indians, who, drunk with victory, had split up into small bands and were raiding small settlements and whites flocking to the Black Hills after the discovery of gold. Martha Jane had fallen in love with a young soldier and rode with the company, which was ordered to join Crook.

General Crook, in command of two thousand men, went out on a trail that led to the southeast, where he expected to join up with General Terry, in command of a larger force and supplies. But Terry failed to arrive and General Crook was reduced to rations for three days. With horses and men weary from marching, the trail led to the Black Hills, about two hundred miles over trails heavy from constant rains. Great suffering was endured. Horses fell by the wayside and the men were foot-sore and weary. Horses and mules unable to keep up were killed to furnish food for the men until a foraging party could be sent out to bring food to the bedraggled and hungry forces.

Major Mills was given command of 150 men. After marching until daybreak he discovered an Indian camp of thirty-five lodges. They hid until night and then attacked the camp. It was a complete surprise to the Indians, bedlam broke loose, and bucks, squaws, and children made a retreat to the hills in the Slim Buttes. A number of Indians were killed, with the loss of only a few soldiers. Fifteen hundred buffalo robes, about three hundred ponies, tons of dried buffalo and deer meat were taken, food that brought joy to the soldiers.

This Indian camp was only a part of the main body of redskins who later arrived with blood-curdling war-whoops. But General Crook, to whom messages had been sent, had arrived and the Indians were whipped. One of General Custer's battle flags was recaptured, also much Seventh Cavalry equipment, proving that this band had been part of the Custer Massacre war party.

General Crook was now supplied with food and went forward with his tattered forces to the Black Hills. There he was received with great joy by the pioneers, who realized the narrow escape they had had.

There Jane was left to mold out her career. Her great boast was that she had been General Crook's scout. At the time she hit Deadwood she was dressed in a soldier's blue uniform and looked like a young boy. She was only sixteen at the time, but looked several years older.

——❧——

Regardless of how small her contribution, Calamity's sojourn into the Black Hills of Dakota Territory only expanded her notoriety. She claimed to have ridden for the Pony Express; she said she had once saved a stagecoach and its six passengers when the driver was killed by Indians; she claimed to have been with Custer immediately before his troops' demise at Little Big Horn. More in keeping with reality, she frequented the saloons, dance halls, and brothels of the Wild West she came to call home. She worked for E.A. Swearingen at his Gem dance hall, which had developed a sordid reputation. Swearingen used to recruit young girls from out East to Deadwood by promising them legitimate, well-paying jobs. Once they stepped off the stage, he laid down the law: "Work for me as a prostitute or you're on your own!" Most often finding themselves broke and hundreds of miles from home, the girls had few options.

For Calamity, if any one town could claim to have been her favorite—like Wyatt Earp carved out Dodge City and Doc Holliday laid claim to Glenwood Springs—it was Deadwood. It's where she felt most comfortable; it's there she felt at home. Whenever she came to town, she got reacquainted with her old "pards," and drank up a storm, gambled, and told tall tales that the locals ate up . Many's the night she stumbled out of a saloon, pistols drawn and firing at the moon following yet another bender. Who—the hard-working, hard-living, hard-playing residents of Deadwood might have asked—wouldn't have just loved her to pieces?

And it was true. By 1877 Calamity had made quite an impression on the locals in the area. The newspapers regularly reported on this new western figure sweeping across the plains. Newspaperman Horatio Nelson Maguire wrote a larger-than-life sketch of Calamity, introducing her to his world. Other newspapers picked up the story (a common practice in the Old West) and reprinted it word for word in their own publications. More than any other writer, Maguire influenced the early legendary feats of Calamity Jane and helped launch her career skyward.

There was nothing in her attire to distinguish her sex, as she sat astride her fiery horse . . . save her small, neat-fitting gaiters and sweeping raven locks. She wore . . . buckskin, gaily beaded and fringed . . . and a broad-brimmed Spanish hat. . . . She comes from Virginia City, Nev. a family of respectability and intelligence. . . . Donning male attire in the mining regions, where no restraints were imposed for such freaks . . . she "took to the road," and has ever since been nomadic in her habits—now one of a hunting party, then participating in a mining stampede, again attached to and moving with a freight train; and, it is said, she has rendered service as a scout. . . . She has had experience as a stage-driver, and can draw the reins over six horses . . . and handles the revolver with dexterity, and fires it as accurately as a Texas ranger. She is still in early womanhood, and her rough and dissipated career has not altogether "swept away the lines where beauty lingers."

The "beauty" to which he alluded wasn't universally acknowledged; but it was there. Scrape away the paint and the mud and the cynicism and the swollen features from alcoholic poisoning, and deep down below was what many would call, if not a *beautiful* woman, at least a *handsome* one. The fact that descriptions of her personal appearance varied tremendously were due to a number of reasons: How old was she at the time? How old and frustrated was the male reporting on her? And just how often (if ever) did the describer see her in person? Oftentimes, writers describing her beauty did so out of a desire to build her into a magnificent creature of the plains more than to accurately describe her attributes. And to build their own readers' following, of course!

While some journalists, such as Maguire, described her as *beautiful,* other newspaper reporters weren't so sympathetic. Clark Tingley, who had seen her in 1875, told a newspaper reporter, "She chews tobacco like an old timer and spits like a ward politician on election day." He added that she was the "hardest case he had ever met in the form of a woman."

Mont Hawthorne, who shared the trail with Calamity in 1877, described her as looking like a "busted bale of hay," claiming she drank too much and talked too much and let her chewing tobacco "get away from her."

Although Maguire may have exaggerated a bit, he wasn't far from wrong when he said she was "mistress of her own destiny." He recognized early on how one of America's earliest female suffragettes elected "to stand alone in brave defiance to a frowning world."

While Calamity had adopted Deadwood as her home, she often traveled to visit her sister, Lena, at the Borner ranch. Borner's family history shows that Lena's second child, Tobias, was born on May 20, 1877. Later in life, "Toby" said he recalled his mother telling him that Aunt Martha had come to help her out after the delivery—something Calamity failed to mention in her autobiography. Then again, why would she reference it, since such humanistic behavior did little to advance her reputation as a hard-working, hard-drinking, sharpshooting frontierswoman!

But not even her sister's newborn son could keep Calamity bottled up in one place for long. Two months later, she showed up in Cheyenne and stopped by the local newspaper office. When she found the editor out, she enlisted the help of a passerby to write a note for him upon his return: "Print in the *Leader* that Calamity Jane, the child of the regiment and pioneer white woman of the Black Hills is in Cheyenne, or I'll scalp you, skin you alive, and hang you to a telegraph pole. Do you hear me and don't you forget it. Calamity Jane."

Despite such undeniably brazen assaults upon their profession, some editors actually took a liking to her, making the effort to probe into who she really was and what honestly made her tick. On one of her frequent Deadwood sojourns, one reporter for a North Dakota newspaper wrote that Calamity had returned to the Hills in August, adding, "She waltzes on one leg and polkas on the other in the hurdy-gurdy houses to make her living." He went on to explain the rationale behind her irrational behavior. "At first a waif in a Mormon camp, then she passed through the mining excitements in the West, now a prostitute, now striving to mend her ways, then a scout wearing men's clothes for General Crook, then the lioness of the Hills . . . she deserves kind words rather than reproach."

Such laudatory accounts were rare. Most editors and the reporters working for them preferred to paint Calamity in a broader, more incendiary light. One writer who chose not to was the editor of the *Black Hills Daily Times*, which paid tribute to her by stating the obvious—that she had a large number of friends among its citizens. The paper went on to say that Calamity "possesses so many good and tender qualities of heart that whenever sickness or trouble overtakes her the derogatory elements of her life are not remembered by the thinking portion of our people."

The writer was obviously referring to Martha's notoriety in nursing the victims of the smallpox epidemic in Deadwood back to health, as well as for coming to the aid of a man named Warren who had been stabbed; she likewise doted over him until his wounds were healed. Of Warren's plight, the local paper took special notice: "There's lots of humanity in Calamity, and she is deserving of much praise for the part she has taken in this particular case."

Some editors, like Alice Gossage of the *Rapid City Daily Journal*, swore never to record the name of Calamity Jane in their pages—*ever!* The effects on Calamity's psyche seemed minimal:

I remained around Deadwood locating claims, going from camp to camp until the spring of 1877, where one morning, I saddled my horse and rode towards Crook city. I had gone about twelve miles from Deadwood, at the mouth of Whitewood creek, when I met the overland mail running from Cheyenne to Deadwood. The horses on a run, about two hundred yards from the station; upon looking closely I saw they were pursued by Indians. The horses ran to the barn as was their custom. As the horses stopped I rode along side of the coach and found the driver John Slaughter, lying face downwards in the boot of the stage, he having been shot by the Indians. When the stage got to the station the Indians hid in the bushes. I immediately removed all baggage from the coach except the mail. I then took the driver's seat and with all haste drove to Deadwood, carrying the six passengers and the dead driver. I left Deadwood in the fall of 1877, and went to Bear Butte Creek with the 7th Cavalry. During the fall and winter we built Fort Meade and the town of Sturgis. In 1878 I left the command and went to Rapid City and put in the year prospecting.

Fact or fiction? It's impossible to tell, although no credible record of Calamity's prospecting in Rapid City or anywhere else exists. Similarly, although her nephew Frank Borner had been born on November 16, 1878, only speculation places her in Lander around that time. Likewise, a paucity of evidence exists that she ever participated in the construction of Fort Meade, although numerous records confirm that she was likely dancing at the saloons in Sturgis around that time. In fact, she had been complimented in one local paper as being "Queen of the Demi Monde" at the Scooptown (Sturgis) dance hall.

Other fanciful but likewise doubtful stories about Calamity had her relaxing on a steamboat navigating up the Missouri River in 1879. A Yankton, Dakota Territory, paper, the *Yankton Press*, noted that Calamity

Jane, a "Black Hills" character, was a passenger on the steamer *Dacotah* en route to the Hills via Fort Pierre. The paper wrote that she had sold her Black Hills mining claim for sixteen thousand dollars and intended to use the money to purchase a ranch. From Fort Pierre, stories had her traveling by stage or freight wagon to Deadwood and up into the Black Hills. Strangely, though, if it's true, Calamity never mentioned any of it, never filed a claim, and never left a record of ever having owned a ranch in the Black Hills.

Despite such discrepancies—or perhaps rather *because* of them—Calamity's support within the local communities continued to grow. One of those supporters, Rolf Johnson, saw Calamity in Deadwood while touring the town in July 1879. He said:

> *Jane is a hard customer and travels on her muscle. She is very handy with either fists or pistols and it takes a good man to get away with her. In the course of the evening I saw her "stand off" with a beer glass a big burley bullwhacker called Taylor, who was drunk and tried to impose on her.*

Johnson ran into Calamity again the following month, recalling that she was "having a fit" after one of the Bismarck freighters tipped over, resulting in two wagons of flour and grain dumping their loads into Whitewood Creek. According to Johnson, she cursed the bullwhacker for the accident, calling him "a 'tender foot'" and cussing him down, saying that if she couldn't do a better job of driving herself, she "would go back to the states and husk pumpkins for a living."

Her own autobiographical record of the incident was considerably more sedate:

> *In 1879 I went to Fort Pierre and drove trains from Rapid City to Fort Pierre for Frank Wife then drove teams from Fort Pierre to Sturgis for Fred Evans. This teaming was done with oxen for they were better fitted for the work than horses, owing to the rough nature of the country.*

So far as being there at the time, several people reported seeing Calamity in Fort Pierre, as her autobiography said. Whether or not she drove teams for freighters is open to debate, although there is no speculation over whether or not she could handle a whip and drive a team as well as or better than any man. White Eye Anderson, a Deadwood acquaintance, recalled that, by using a whip and a lot of cussing, she could goad the teams over the roughest of terrain. Anderson also acknowledged that she could shoot a rifle or her six-shooters with equal deadly accuracy.

Larger than life? That was her persona. And it was not without basis in fact. Anyone who saw her in person could never forget the first impression she made. Several witnesses recorded seeing her on the Fort Pierre trail. A Black Hills pioneer recalled his impressions of her:

> *I met her in '79. . . . I was coming in and Calamity was going out and our wagons camped together about the first night out of Pierre. I said who is that loud-mouthed man and the boss said, "That ain't no man that's Calamity Jane." She stood in the middle of a great circle and cracked the bullwhip. Nobody could crack a whip like Calamity Jane. I never heard anything like it. When she made a right good crack they whooped and hollered and stopped for a drink. They just plain raised the devil around that camp.*

Another man, Jack Sutley, who operated a road ranch on the Fort Pierre–to–Deadwood Trail, recalled hearing a knock on the door one night. When he opened it, his eyes fell upon none other than Calamity Jane. She asked for asylum from a U.S. marshal, who was pursuing her for selling whiskey without a government license. Not wishing to run afoul of John Law, himself, Sutley advised her to cross the river and join the freighters, who were her friends and sure to hide her out. He lent Calamity a horse—a good swimmer, but one that had developed the nasty habit of shaking the water off its body after crossing a river. Sutley said later he could tell that Calamity had made the crossing successfully when he heard a full line of expletives leveled at the animal from the other side.

While in Fort Pierre, Calamity was alleged to have been an associate of the scourge of the territory, a man named Arkansaw Putello. A fellow freighter and a bad-tempered drunk, he terrorized the town's "decent folk" whenever he went on a bender. Legendary for his prowess with a gun, he often took potshots at the town's honest citizens, as well as anyone unfortunate enough to be traveling the roads into town. He never killed any of *them*, although he *did* once kill an outlaw, as well as the man's brother-in-law. The town citizens organized a vigilante committee to confront him and force him to change his ways, but to no avail.

After he killed the bandit Texas George, who had harassed the area for years, the citizens felt grateful enough for his help to make a gift to him of a horse, a saddle, and a head start out of town. Instead, Arkansaw sold the horse and saddle and was said to have blown the money drinking at a local saloon with Calamity and several like-minded "associates."

In another incident, Calamity, George Baker, and several others had decided to pool their savings and open a bagnio, or a whorehouse, at the end of the Northwestern tracks some sixty miles east of town. The citizens raised such a ruckus, though, that Baker was eventually shot, although not fatally. Calamity soon gave up the notion.

Despite incidents such as those, Calam's rough-and-tumble ways and shady reputation were reputed to be little more than a cover for the warmth and generosity she showed toward her fellow travelers through life. Everyone in Fort Pierre knew by heart the story of her nursing a local family with black diphtheria back to health, spending her own money to buy groceries and medicine. The family pledged their undying gratitude to Martha Jane. And that was enough to convince the people of Fort Pierre that the woman's life in reality transcended her reputation.

No matter *what* anyone else might have said about her.

But, for Calamity, life was just beginning, and the big bad world was still out there, waiting to be conquered.

CHAPTER SEVEN

Wyoming and the Union Pacific

This schoolhouse was built by John Borner along the Old Indian Trail near the mouth of Sinks Canyon. Mr. Borner was well known by residents of Lander for his large, plentiful garden. He was married in 1875 to Lena (Jenny) Canary, the sister of the legendary Calamity Jane.

—PLACARD ERECTED BY THE MUSEUM OF THE AMERICAN WEST, LANDER, WYOMING

MARTHA JANE CANNARY FLITTED LIKE A HONEYBEE FROM ONE POLLEN-laden flower to the next, from one frontier town to another; but she always landed back in Lander. That was her second home, after Deadwood. After all, sister Lena and her sister's family lived there. Usually she'd visit on her own; occasionally, she'd bring Elijah. The newspapers mentioned her name whenever she showed up in town.

Calamity's new nephew, Frank Edward Borner, was born to Lena and her husband on November 16, 1878. Later, he recalled ducking behind his mother's skirts whenever a woman rode up to the porch of their cabin. Eventually he learned the woman was his Aunt Calam.

Most of the early visits with the Borners were cordial, warm, and even loving. One was not. Lena's husband, John, had gotten wind of his sister-in-law's hijinks. On that particular day, when Calamity rode up, Lena rushed out onto the porch with Frank right behind her. She warned Martha to turn around and ride off, and Frank thought it was because of his aunt's rough ways and crude talk. And in a way he was right.

John Borner had decided that, now that he and his wife had a family to raise, they needed to protect their children from Calamity's drinking, cursing, and whoring around. Regardless, Borner's new attitude toward Calamity merely sent the frontierswoman sneaking in the back door. Whenever she got wind that Borner was away from home, Calamity stole out to the ranch for a visit. One of the Borners' neighbors, Ernest Hornecker, admitted to seeing her pass by in a buggy on her way to the Borner place whenever John was away. Tom Bell, a local historian, confirmed that Calamity stayed at the Borner School when she came to visit her sister, since her brother-in-law had forbidden her to set foot in their home.

Despite Calamity's crudeness, she had a soft spot in her heart for young children—perhaps because fate had robbed her of her own childhood years. Estelline Bennett, a youngster growing up in Deadwood at the time, recalled the plainswoman offering to buy some candy for her and her friend, Maude. Estelline confessed she was shaking in her boots, almost too frightened to take Calamity up on the offer. *Almost.* Years later, she remembered that Calamity had thrown a silver dollar onto the counter, ordering the owner to give the girls as "much as they kin eat!"

Amy McGuire, who also remembered Calamity in the old days, wrote a tribute to her after Calamity had passed on: "She was a lover of children and a suppliant for their favor" who periodically offered to buy them candy, although some of their mothers ordered them to give it back. A few town women who felt sorry for Calamity occasionally allowed her to hold their infants.

Of course, Calamity wasn't always so well behaved. An undated incident in Lander only served to solidify Borner's opinion of her. When his sister-in-law became so drunk one day that she stripped off all her clothes and began singing at the "top of her lungs" while parading up and down Main Street, local authorities arrested her. Much to Borner's chagrin, they brought her out to his ranch for the Borners to deal with while she sobered up.

For a good many years, Calamity—like Blanche DuBois in later literature—relied upon the kindness of strangers. Often, the "strangers" were the workers at the Union Pacific Railroad. Taking on a job, she worked side by side with the toughest of them, often, according to local accounts, putting them to shame. At the end of the day, she quenched her thirst for both alcohol and adventure in one of the many small-town saloons that had sprouted up along the railroad line. The hamlets of Cheyenne, Laramie, Rawlins, and Green River could all lay claim to the fact that "Calamity Jane once slept here." Never mind that she more appropriately slept it *off* there!

Calamity's dalliance with members of the opposite gender—not to mention her reliance upon their vices—understandably put off a number of local women. Many of the ragtag "towns" were barely worthy of the name. More like makeshift settlements thrown together out of the necessity of railroading for a living, these places were often barren and desolate—dry as the dust blowing across them from the west in the summers and wet as a mud hen during the rainy season in spring. Saloons were among the first to sprout because they were among the easiest of business establishments to found and grow in such wild and wooly environments. Laws were few and far between. Often, they were nonexistent. Animals shared the streets with people, rendering the roadways filthy and ugly. Hoodlums and outlaws roamed back and forth between the towns, although strangely enough they never seemed to bother Calamity. She had long since proven she could hold her own and often joined them at the bars, participating in their drunken revelry. If anyone made fun of her or, God forbid, of the crude manner in which she talked, she simply pulled out her pistols and laid them on the bar. Unlike most "civilized" folks of the era, Calamity thrived on the desolate discards of polite society as readily as others spat on and cursed them.

By the 1880s, railroad construction was booming—good news for everyone who ever needed a job, including Martha Jane Cannary. Since many of the towns were connected by other lines and short spurs, Calamity found the previously daunting task of traveling around the countryside easier than ever, taking advantage of every opportunity that travel by rail offered.

Somehow, she always seemed to scrape enough money together to buy a ticket to somewhere else whenever her life in one town or another began to grow old. But not always.

During one of those nights when she had visited one bar too many, whooping and hollering and raising holy hell, she passed out; and as one resident of Horr, Montana, recalled, her friends simply called for a wagon to pick her up and take her to the depot. There she slept until the train arrived, after which two railroaders grabbed her by the legs and the arms and swung her like a slab of beef into the open door of the baggage car. She woke up headed to yet another adventure.

It wasn't the first time; it wouldn't be the last.

But as simple as travel by rail had become, even for people who hopped onboard cold sober, it was not always a viable means of transportation. Since railroads came only within thirty-seven miles of Lander and her sister's home, Calamity's visits gradually faded to a precious few. When Lena gave birth to her daughter, Theresa Theodosha, in 1880, Calamity passed up the opportunity of wishing mother and daughter well, opting instead to spend that time in Fort Pierre and Rapid City.

Still, the following year, on April 26, 1881, sometime after Lena had given birth to a second daughter, Calamity found a way to make it to the Borner home once more. Her visit was immensely successful: She had, in a relatively short period of time, taught her new niece to mimic Aunt Calam's cursing, lending even more fuel to the flames already burning within her brother-in-law's heart.

Perhaps it was all the domesticity she found in her sister—or maybe it was simply Father Time taking hold of the reins—but for whatever reason, Calamity reached a point in her life when she began thinking seriously about changing her ways and settling down. In 1882, while living on a ranch near Miles City with a man she called her *husband* by title if not by ceremony, Calamity gave birth to a son whom she named Little Calamity. She assured the local newspaper "that she had been entirely regenerated and that during the balance of her days she intended to lead a quiet, domestic . . . life, visiting town only occasionally to hear the band play." Perhaps she was honest in her intent. She had attended the opera in Bismarck, North Dakota, earlier in the year and had generated news headlines as that woman "of the Black Hills notoriety."

However, in the end, Calamity was only deluding herself. Little Calamity died from unknown causes, and she returned to her old ways. In

November 1882 she was said to be "doing business at Billings," according to the *Weekly Register Call*. She reportedly had transferred her unspecified "business" somewhere up-valley from town, the paper noting that "Billings does not regret her loss as any great calamity either."

By December, the *Register Call* reported that Martha Jane had returned to her fallback line of work: "Calamity Jane has gone back on the turf and is running a hurdy-gurdy house at Livingston."

Calamity recalled:

In 1881 I went to Wyoming and returned in 1882 to Miles City and took up a ranch on the Yellow Stone, raising stock and cattle, also kept a way side inn, where the weary traveler could be accommodated with food, drink, or trouble if he looked for it. Left the ranch in 1883, went to California, going through the States and territories, reached Ogden around the latter part of 1883, and San Francisco in 1884.

She never mentioned her alleged "husband" in her autobiographical entry, and she avoided using the plural pronoun *we*. In fact, she rarely mentioned a traveling companion at all. The man she lived with on the ranch might have been Frank King, who was most likely the father of Little Calamity. She did adopt the name of Mattie King for a while, lending an additional air of legitimacy to her relationship.

In 1883, as she admitted, she left the ranch for California but was forced by the weather to settle for the winter in Montana where she was arrested with a man named Kibble for selling liquor to the Indians on the Camas Prairie. She and Kibble served time in a jail in Missoula.

That spring, Calamity did indeed press on to the West Coast. About that time, another railroad was being built—this one through the northwest; along with it came the usually predictable string of tent cities, camps, and wilderness settlements. Naturally, with the railroads, the usual plethora of workers rushed to town and, with them, an influx of fresh cash. Opportunity knocked once more, and Calamity was quick to answer.

Wide open and wild, the West Coast provided Martha an opportunity to spread her wings. She lived in Spokane for a short while, dealing faro in a wooden building on Maine Avenue, next to the place where the

Owl Saloon would eventually be constructed. While dealing, she chewed tobacco, smoked cigars, and drank whiskey like a man—all the more endearing her to the rowdies and roughnecks in the vicinity. She stayed until wanderlust struck once again, and she headed off to the gold strikes during the rush in the Coeur d'Alenes, Idaho.

Although Calamity claimed to have been in Texas in 1884, the newspapers pinned her down in Idaho and Wyoming during that time. One article from March 27, 1884, confirmed that "Calamity Jane, the most noted woman of the western frontier and the heroine of many a thrilling nickel novel, has pulled up stakes and joined the stampede for the Coeur d'Alenes."

Various other papers reported her trip to Coeur d'Alenes in 1884. A Black Hills wag noted her departure, adding, "Poor old Calam has been the most unfortunate woman that ever struck this country.... Three years ago she married and settled down on a ranch near Miles City, and has remained there ever since, and is an honored member of the Miles City Society."

Not too far away, a Montana paper found Calamity living in Livingston, another town along the Northern Pacific line and a locale that Calamity enjoyed haunting. "Jane has been living down the valley for some time but has pulled up stakes and joined the stampede for the Coeur d'Alenes." Not long after, Calamity returned to Deadwood where she stayed for a short period before moving back to Livingston. There, the papers noted, "Jane has successfully escaped various trials and tribulations incident to a trip to the Coeur d'Alenes and is back in Livingston again. She has had enough of the mines and abused that country in round terms. Jane has had a life's experiences in western camps, and is able to size up a new country pretty intelligently."

Calamity visited Eagle City, a short-lived boomtown, on her first trip to the Coeur d'Alenes. Enjoying the rough-and-tumble atmosphere of the town, which began as a tent city in 1883, she drank and hollered and shot her way there into infamy. But even her stay there was short-lived. By August of the following year, the gold had run out, and the population had just as quickly dwindled to a few stubborn stragglers.

Uncharacteristically, Calamity undertook the arduous trip to Eagle City accompanied by an entourage of eight women, all traveling by horseback over the rugged Jackass Trail, straddling the Continental Divide in the Wind River Mountains. A tough trek even for a sure-footed donkey, the steep, granite inclines proved nearly impenetrable for their horses, not to mention the female riders aboard them.

But in the end, all nine women arrived safely and found themselves the stars of the biggest shindig ever to hit Eagle City. One newspaper article reported that the first big social event of the year—and probably *ever!*—took place in the Murray District north of Wallace in 1884. Calamity and her girls took over a tented barroom to dance, drink, party, and in whatever other ways they could think, entertain their clientele, nearly exclusively male. Adam Aulbach, editor of a local newspaper, wrote, "As red calico stage curtains parted, in her mannish woolens, [Calamity] did a monologue of her life. The girls, more feminine, danced and the party was on." Each man chose his favorite gal, and they took a few turns around the floor. By the time the evening had ended, a string of fights had erupted and some raucous gunplay had ensued; but by the following morning, Calamity was left standing, counting her profits.

When Calamity returned to Montana, the *Billings Post* reported that she had left on Monday's train to join the Liver-Eating Johnson Expedition. The paper also noted that she wasn't as attractive in appearance as she had been in her earlier days in Deadwood.

"The erratic female, known as Calamity Jane," the paper said, "who was one of the first stampeders into the Black Hills Country left on Monday's train to join the Liver-Eating Johnson Troupe."

But that turned out to be only the beginning of the tale. Calamity had been eyeing a much more profitable future than bouncing from town to town, taking up patrons' offers to buy her drinks . . . and sometimes more. She had slowly but steadily become aware of a new offing on the horizon. It was time that Calamity Jane begun saddling up to *real* notoriety.

Throughout the 1880s, a number of traveling shows had been springing up around the country. Designed to recall the glory days of the Old

West, the open-air touring performances of Buffalo Bill Cody, Pawnee Bill, and Doc Carver proved wildly popular wherever they traveled. The Liver-Eating Johnson Troupe was built around a man who allegedly ate the livers of the Crow Indians he killed after they had murdered his family. Johnson was joined in the show by former western army scouts; Crow Indians; Curley, alleged to be the sole survivor of the Battle of the Little Big Horn; and, of course, Calamity Jane. After a few months, financial troubles put an end to the show, and most members were forced to sell their ponies in order to get back to Montana.

As newsworthy as this experience would have been, Calamity nevertheless failed to mention her participation in the show in her autobiography, saying instead only that:

Left San Francisco in the summer of 1884 for Texas, stopping at Fort Yuma, Arizona, the hottest spot in the United States. Stopping at all points of interest until I reached El Paso in the fall. While in El Paso, I met Mr. Clinton Burk, a native of Texas, who I married in August of 1885. As I thought I had traveled through life long enough alone and thought it was about time to take a partner for the rest of my days.

Calamity's recollection of her new husband was scarred on several counts. First, his name was Clinton *Burke*. Second, she never met him on the date she specified. In fact, she had spent 1885 in Wyoming, taking time out to visit her sister in Lander from time to time, and even living there for a short while before wearing out her welcome and moving on.

During November 1884, Calamity found herself in Wyoming where she was reported to have been "leading a quiet life at Fort Washakie." Since she was already in the vicinity, she most likely worked in a short trip to Lander to see Lena and Calam's new niece, Bertha (Bertie Pauline), born in September 1884.

But in her inimitable style, Martha Jane was off again nearly as quickly as she had come. In December, she was back in Rawlins, Wyoming: "Calamity Jane the noted and notorious . . . is in Rawlins," a Wyoming newspaper reported. Calamity railed back and forth among various Wyoming towns for the next ten years, most often wearing out her welcome wherever she went. Still, she stayed fairly close to "home," wherever she felt that might have been, visiting Lander in 1885, in between several jaunts to Rawlins. Caught in Lander by a reporter, she spurred the man to declare quite uncharitably, "Calamity Jane, who infested the Yellowstone Valley a few years ago, is said to be disporting herself among the residents of Lander, Wyoming."

When Lena gave birth to Calam's latest nephew, William Frederick, on April 27, 1885, Calamity took advantage of visiting her family as often as she could, which meant whenever Borner was away. While in Lander, Calamity was profiled in "A Sketch of the Reckless Life of This Female Bandit." The newspaper reported: "A correspondent of the *Cheyenne Leader,* writing from Lander, Wyo., under date of Oct 30th, gives the following account of a peculiar character whose history begins in Uinta County [in Utah]." The sketch went on to describe her. "She owned the heart of a tigress. Reckless in disposition, pretty in looks, and full of animal spirits, she had lovers by the crowd." The interview began with her early life when Calamity was in the company of the Gallaghers in Miner's Delight in 1868 and concluded with her supposed association with the Bevan's gang, a group of outlaws staging daring raids during the period. According to the interview, Calamity supposedly laid the plan for a bold stagecoach robbery in 1877, even though she was never proven to have been involved in that or any other organized criminal activities.

Confirming her presence in Lander, a Bismarck, North Dakota, newspaper reported in November 1885 that Calamity Jane was "terrorizing Lander City at present."

During the fall and winter of that year, Calamity continued bouncing between Lander and Rawlins. Wyoming newspapers reported that she was in Rawlins in the earlier part of November. "Calamity is here, but she came on the coach, she may be found in a neat little, rough board one-room residence on Slaughterhouse street." One week later, she was reported to have settled in Lander.

The following year, Calamity found herself among the society notes in the Rawlins newspaper in July 1886. "It is the proper thing to remark that Calamity Jane has been painting the town in her usual lurid style during the week. She dropped in from Idaho."

At some point, Calamity met and joined forces with a man named Bill Steers. He was nine years younger and possessed an abusive disposition toward her. They may have met in Rawlins and traveled together to Meeker, Colorado. Several years before, the Colorado White River Indian Agency had experienced the Ute uprising of 1879 and the Ute War of 1880. The resulting legislation by Congress moved the Utes to reservations. A garrison called Camp at White River was built and populated on the future site of Meeker, which was founded after the troops left the fort in 1883.

According to a Meeker-area resident, Calamity and her "husband" lived together for two months or more. Then, in September, Calamity swore out a warrant for Steers's arrest. He had taken after her with a knife and assaulted her with a rock on her lip. After several days in jail, Steers endured a quick trial, following which he and Calamity buried the hatchet, celebrating by getting drunk at the nearest saloon. The next day, she apparently forgave him, and they left Meeker together. But all was not roses for the Steers family.

That fall of 1886 Calamity traveled to Rawlins after Steers's trial. The newspaper announced her presence as using the name Mrs. Mattie King at the post office. The local reporter, in a stretch of benevolence toward her, wrote, "Calamity is not half as bad as the human ghouls that abuse her. The victim of passion, with generous impulses, this poor pilgrim has been made the scapegoat of the outlaw, the assassin, the tinhorn, and at last the outcast of man." Another newspaper added that, in their opinion, Steers deserved "a hangman's knot."

Regardless, the following month, it was Calamity who wound up behind bars, this time in the Rawlins County Jail. She and Steers had gotten into another fight after Steers, whom the reporter described as "one of the most worthless curs unhung," had taken a wrench and slammed it across Calamity's head. The blow left a large gash. When Calamity failed to receive the sort of sympathy she thought she should have elicited from a local saloon, she picked up a rock and hurled it through a large glass window. Steers managed to escape apprehension, although he was caught shortly thereafter and jailed for thirty days for assault. The Rawlins newspaper—still clearly behind Calamity—wrote that it was time Steers received the full weight of the law: "He is a miserable stick and deserves a more severe punishment than a month's free board, but the law will not allow it."

In March 1887 Calamity popped up in Cheyenne after more than a decade's absence. Some reports say she appeared to be in terrible physical condition, partly, no doubt, due to Steers. While in town, a reporter from the *Cheyenne Daily Leader* interviewed Calamity in July 1887. As was by then the norm, her life's story wandered all over the place as she painted herself to be the unsung hero of every extraordinary situation to have unfolded west of the Mississippi. She told the paper she was born of poor parents at Fort Washakie and was "adopted into the family of an officer stationed there, but ran away and entered upon a 'sporting' life at the age of thirteen years."

She continued with numerous other outlandish tales that had her ranging from Cheyenne and Lander to Rawlins and Deadwood. In all of them, she made herself the center of attention.

In Bismarck, she claimed, two army officers had fought "on her account." One of them was killed, and she had to leave town to escape a mob out to lynch her. After settling in Lander, she claimed, "a drunken cowboy had killed a store keeper" on her account. Calamity, overwhelmed by empathy, concluded that she was sorry, but she "could not help it."

The article wrapped up with the announcement that Calamity had married Mr. Steers two years prior and had been living a reasonably quiet life, except for her sprees.

Unfortunately for the truth, she was not married to Steers at the time she claimed to be. In fact, she was in Lander in August 1887, as the press so dutifully reported: "The only and original Calamity Jane is now in Lander, and is improving Lander influence by leading a strictly, industrious and happy life."

But the papers, as usual, bit on Calam's tales hook, line, and sinker. The September 2, 1887, edition of the *Leader* announced, "Wm. P. Steers is the husband of the famous Calamity Jane. The pair now resides at Lander, Fremont County."

In reality, the couple didn't marry until May 30, 1888, in Pocatello, but that didn't stop Calamity from claiming to be Steers's wife. Her illegitimate child, Jessie, needed a father—even if in name only.

Not long after, the *Sundance Gazette* ran an erroneous article saying that Calamity was married to William P. Steers: "Steers recently wrote a letter to a friend in this city in which he states has succeeded in 'getting away with the old woman's watch and chain.' Steers and Calamity separate about four times every year, and as often reunite. The dime-novel heroine's husband is a lightly built, sickly looking and unassuming genius, about 25 years old. He was born in the backwoods of Wisconsin."

Confounding matters further, Calamity claimed in her autobiography that she and her alleged husband, Clinton Burke, were in Texas until 1889.

We remained in Texas leading a quiet home life until 1889. On October 28th, 1887, I became the mother of a girl baby, the very image of its father, at least that is what he said, but who has the temper of its mother.

Why the subterfuge? Calamity, in a desperate effort to begin her daughter's life without the stain of the mother's sins attached to her, wanted people to know that Clinton Burke and not William Steers was the baby's father, although, in all likelihood, the real father was Bill Steers. Presumably, the baby girl was born in Lander, possibly with the help of Martha Jane's sister, Lena.

Unlike Martha Jane, Lena was perfectly happy being a housewife and mother. To her, roots were important. Still, she recognized that the time was right to relocate. Regardless, she realized that, wherever the Borner family settled, she would have plenty of work to do, between raising their children—now numbering seven—and caring for their new homestead.

Jane, of course, was just the opposite. She had grown from a wandering youngster on the open plains into a pulp-novel heroine of exploding stature. And it was nearly all due to a man by the name of Deadwood Dick.

The hero of a series of stories, called dime novels, appearing between 1877 and 1897, Deadwood Dick was the featured character of the most outrageous western adventures by an intrepid fictional hero. At first the Deadwood Dick series did just fine on its own. But then its creator, a man named Edward Lytton Wheeler, began hearing tall tales about a real-life woman named Calamity Jane. He soon got the notion of playing Jane off of Dick to double up on his readers' satisfaction, not to mention their numbers. It was a means to attract more female readers to the series! And it worked. In fact, the installments were so popular that, before long, various real-life westerners took on the names of Deadwood Dick and Calamity Jane. Two of the more notorious appropriators of the Deadwood Dick moniker were a man named Richard Palmer, who died in Cripple Creek, Colorado, in 1906, and Robert "Deadeye Dick" Dickey, who died in a Denver hospital jail in 1912.

The popular syndicated television series *Death Valley Days* presented a 1966 episode entitled "The Resurrection of Deadwood Dick," hosted by Robert Taylor. The lead role was played by actor Denver Pyle.

Very little of what Wheeler wrote in his novels was true, but that didn't matter to a growing legion of Deadwood Dick and Calamity Jane fans. As long as there was a story to tell, Jane was quick to tell it—the more embellishment the better, so far as she was concerned. And she quickly realized that her fans felt the same.

Roughly ten years after the Deadwood Dick series made its debut, two writers by the names of Street and Smith of the *New York Weekly* placed an ad announcing a story entitled *Calamity Jane, The Queen of the Plains: A Tale of Daring Deeds by a Brave Woman's Hands*. Promoted as being written by a contributor named Reckless Ralph, a great trapper and hunter who lived among the scenes he described, the first chapters appeared as a serial in January 1888 in the *Weekly*. Finally, readers' could satisfy their insatiable appetites for Wild Western bravado by subscribing to the series and reading about the thrilling exploits of Calamity Jane and all the highwaymen, gold diggers, desperadoes, and Indians she fought off.

At the same time, real life for Martha Jane was nowhere near so idyllic or exciting. She was having ongoing difficulties with Steers. Not to be outdone, Lena and her husband were having problems of their own. On February 23, 1888, the *Freemont Clipper* reported a conflict over an irrigation ditch that Lena had decided to build. The ditch began funneling water to the Borner ranch at the expense of their neighbors, who took the Borners to court. The commissioners turned the case over to a trio of appraisers who were to assess the damages to the neighboring landowners, Hornecker and Nicol. It all came about after Lena Borner had constructed a ditch on the Borners' property in order to reclaim eighty-nine acres of desert land. Once completed, the ditch was to be nearly three miles long, with several above-ground flumes. The entire project was predicted to cost nearly eight hundred dollars, an extraordinary figure for the time.

The river Lena tapped ran full of water, which the farmers diverted fairly equally by the construction of various ditches to water their crops. When Lena attempted to divert so much water for the Borners' personal use, the community rebelled.

The dispute continued into March 1888, when the *Freemont Clipper* reported the court's findings: "The damage assessed against Mrs. Lena Borner on account of the ditch was placed at $114, which the aggrieved parties refuse to accept. Mrs. Borner will proceed with the ditch pending further litigation." Meanwhile, her husband, John, who was out scouting locations for a new homestead for his family on the present site of Greybull, Wyoming, knew little of what was going on at home.

When Borner finally returned to Lander that June, he learned what had happened. By then, the ditch was completed. Just about the time he planned on opening the flume to let the water in, he discovered that someone had cut into it with a secondary flume, diverting the water to J. M. Hornecker's neighboring farm "and at a point where the latter's ditch crosses it."

Borner proceeded with an injunction to prevent further interference, launching legal action against Hornecker for destruction of private property.

But their legal problems weren't the worst of the Borners nightmares. Earlier, while Borner was away in Billings on his annual trip for supplies, Lena was feeding a calf tied to a post when she became entangled in the rope tied to the calf. She tripped, fell, and injured her hip, which caused an abscess that she ignored. At the height of the Borners' legal battle over water rights, the abscess exploded, and Lena died. Borner and the children were devastated. The obituary in the local paper read:

At Rest. Late on Saturday, when twilight shadows began to veil the quiet earth, Lena, the beloved wife of John G. Borner, closed her eyes on the misty sights of earth and sank into the dreamless sleep of eternity. Her death is a sad blow to her husband, and the entire community gives him its full sympathy in his deep affliction. Seven little children, the oldest but ten years of age, are left to his care and guidance. Mrs. Borner had been in ill health for some time, and never recovered from an accident that befell her two years ago. She was one of the most industrious women in the valley and one whom all her acquaintances held in the highest respect. Her pride was in her children and her home and her hands were ever busy with the work they found to do. All that medical skill could accomplish was done for her, but the unrelenting shadow of death had settled upon her, and her system, worn down by patient toil and cares, gave way beneath the unequal strain. Her funeral, which was largely attended took place yesterday, Rev. Frank M. Day officiating, the burial occurring in the Masonic cemetery at North Fork. J. I. Patten, E.F Cheney, Chas. E. Fogg, FG. Burnett, Charley Allen, and Samuel Sparhawk were the pall bearers. Undertaker Firestone had charge of the ceremony.

As if that news wasn't bad enough for Calamity—who had nurtured and fretted over the welfare of her baby sister—she was still entangled with Steers. In April 1888 *Buffalo's Big Horn Sentinel* reported that Calamity had her "so-called husband arrested for assault and thrown in jail at Green River." Later, she, too, was arrested for intoxication and disorderly conduct. The reporter wrote that she "now occupies quarters in the county bastile [sic]." A week later, the *Sundance Gazette* substantiated the report, adding, "That noted character 'Calamity Jane' was given four hours at Green River, Wyoming to rustle a fine or leave town. She skipped."

As strange as it seems, her continuing battles with Steers weren't enough to dissuade Calamity from marrying him—most certainly in a vain attempt to protect her daughter, Jessie, from vicious gossip as the child grew up. So, on May 30, 1888, she and Steers went to Pocatello, Idaho, where they were married before local witnesses Lizzie Bard and Charles Brown.

It's not clear whether or not Calamity expected that piece of legality to solve all her problems, but it is clear that it didn't. As the New Year, 1888/89, approached, Calamity set out to Wendover, Wyoming, alone. The *Cheyenne Weekly Sun* reported, "Calamity is the most amiable of women; ornery of feature though kindly of eye, and an enthusiastic bull on the whiskey market. . . . As a female holy terror she has no living superior, and her worst enemies will not deny that she is an able drinker."

The following June, Calamity left with her husband for Oakland, California, according to a San Francisco newspaper. They most likely had with them their daughter, Jessie, and two "adopted sons" whom A. C. Warren had entrusted to Calamity after his wife had left him and Warren had no way of caring for them. But following one of their frequent battles, Steers once again betrayed Calamity in a letter he wrote to Warren, claiming—not too unjustly—that Martha was an unfit guardian because she was a drunk. Concerned for the welfare of his children, Warren rushed to Oakland and immediately filed papers with the court to petition for custody of his boys.

During the legal battle, Martha's husband turned out to be a less-than-supportive witness for the prosecution. When asked if he had been imprisoned several times and was living off of the fallen woman's proceeds, he acknowledged that he was. But even if Steers's history had gone unnoticed by the court, it wasn't so with the press, who published an article coming to Calamity's defense, saying she "has been compelled to support him and endure his cruelty" for most of her married life.

The newspaper went on to explain that Warren had given the child to Martha Steers when she and Steerses were in Tacoma the year before. Warren's wife had left him with three children, and since he wasn't able to care for them, he gave two boys to Martha, who had expressed concern over their well-being. At some point, Warren had enticed the younger boy back and decided to press charges that Martha was keeping the eight-year-old boy against his will.

Acknowledging that Martha Steers was Calamity Jane, the newspaper described her as "a degraded woman with bleary eyes and a dangerous breath." Not long after the testimony, a local sheriff found her lying in a yard "beastly drunk" with the child in her arms before the start of the trial.

The courtroom broke into hysterics when the judge moved to give Warren, the natural father, custody of the child, despite Martha's promises to watch over him and keep him free from harm.

Calamity was in such a state of despair that the judge suggested she be placed under the charge of the Association of Charities. Calamity flatly refused. No mention was made of Jessie, Calam's daughter, age two, during the hearings.

Following the trial, Calamity likely gained a common-law divorce from Steers. One Livingston newspaper alluded to a divorce she obtained "from her second husband" in "Almeda, California." Although *Alameda* is the county in which both Oakland and San Francisco reside, no official divorce record or any court case proceedings exist. But the papers persisted. "I'm a rough woman, jedge," Calamity said, "but these kids alus have had a square deal from me, I ain't no saint, and yet I might be worse; I've nursed this man that's I' this divorce, and I've saved his worthless life once; the law ain't givin' me a square deal—it never gives a woman a square deal, nohow."

Considering the fact that Calamity was herself orphaned at a young age and given every opportunity to "make it" on her own, it's ironic that suddenly she felt herself lacking a "square deal." Or is it?

Calamity Jane was able to survive and prosper in life, even as an orphan at her tender young age, not because of the "square deals" provided to her by society and the law but rather by her own cunning and innate desire to survive. She was able to work her way through the gender-prejudicial Old West not by relying upon the equality of the law but instead by pretending to be someone she wasn't: a man.

Certainly young orphaned males have had an easier time assimilating into western culture than females of the same age. Society looks at females far more protectively—as if they require more "minding" than their male counterparts to keep them safe and free from harm. Whether or not that's a legitimate premise, it certainly existed back in Calamity's time. Furthermore, she instinctively knew it.

How better to avoid being picked up, hauled off to jail for loitering, and shipped off to a home for wayward girls than not to *be a girl*—or, at least, not to be *seen* as a girl? So it appears that many of Calamity Jane's peculiarly masculine habits—smoking, drinking, shooting, cursing, dressing—were less the result of a personal proclivity than an understanding of just what and who she felt she had to be in order to survive.

When we see such a statement as Calamity made in court that day, we get a different view as to why. Calamity's nearly lifelong attempt to be a woman in a man's world was not without its failures. Eventually, she was always discovered to be a woman, no matter how she dressed, talked, or acted. And so being the case, she also experienced another of society's damning tricks: As a woman, she had a limited means of employment available to her. As a man, there were no set limits. So, while she proved to be androgynous, she flew through society with the highest of social and economic potential. But when discovered as a woman, she lost them all and was forced to settle for menial work at minimal pay.

Certainly, she was "discovered as a woman" often enough to have had to dabble in all feminine employment opportunities available to her at the time, from working as an occasional seamstress and cook to toiling away as a cleaning lady, laundress, and even a prostitute. Socially, she was not without feminine charms, even outside the boudoir. She was one of the best hurdy-gurdy dancers in a hall, not to mention one of the highest tip gatherers.

But when push came to shove, she derived little solace in being one of feminism's "best" while slowly going down the tubes to financial ruin for not being even one of masculinity's mediocre specimens. It wasn't Calamity's good looks or dancing skills or nursing prowess that enabled her to survive in a rough-and-tumble male-oriented world. It was her prowess in transforming her work ethic into those of a man. That's what wrested her success from certain failure.

So, shed of her own "man" for good, Calamity returned to Wyoming. Steers most likely stayed on in California and died there in 1933 at the age of sixty-seven.

Undeterred by her split, Calamity drove herself on to several Wyoming towns. She visited Cheyenne in January 1890, arriving from Casper, Wyoming. The papers continued to write about her in a positive light, as did the *Cheyenne Tribune* when it most charitably christened her "the uncrowned queen of a thousand frontier towns and mining camps and who is the heroine of numerous sensational publications." They failed to bring up the subject of Calamity's daughter, Jessie.

Before long, the local newspapers alluded to the fact that Calamity had been "fired out of Cheyenne" and deposited at the doorstep of Casper, but again she failed to dally there long. From Casper she traveled to Laramie on the night's train. There, she retained a relatively low profile, finally moving on to Rock Springs in June 1890, where she arrived under the name of Jane Steers. Laramie was especially attractive to Calam at that time since nine new coal mines had opened in nearby Rock Springs in 1890. New coal mines meant new miners, mostly single, mostly bored, and most definitely hungry for the companionship of an available "lady." To most jaded westerners, Calamity filled the bill. For a while.

Following a trip to Iowa to visit some relatives in 1892, Calamity returned to tell reporters that she had settled down in Lander. But her "settling" didn't last very long. In December 1893 Calamity traveled on to Green River, using the name Mrs. King, offering the plausible explanation that she had recently reunited with her "ex," if only temporarily.

But, true to form, she soon moved again, this time to Billings, Montana, which is where she most likely had originally met Burke.

And her life once more took a dramatic turn. For better . . . or for worse.

"Lower Main Street," Deadwood, South Dakota, 1877, showing the Creedmoor Gunshop, the Meat Market, and other commercial buildings. MONTANA HISTORICAL SOCIETY RESEARCH CENTER PHOTOGRAPH ARCHIVES, HELENA, MT

"Bill Reece's Dance Hall," 1879. View of log building with board-and-batten front in Miles City, Montana, with a carriage, horses, and people in the street. A well appears in front of the hall where Calamity kicked up her heels on more than one occasion. MONTANA HISTORICAL SOCIETY RESEARCH CENTER PHOTOGRAPH ARCHIVES, HELENA, MT

"Calamity Jane," 1880. A studio portrait view of Calamity seated against a typical studio backdrop. MONTANA HISTORICAL SOCIETY RESEARCH CENTER PHOTOGRAPH ARCHIVES, HELENA, MT

"Northern Pacific" railroad depot and yard, Miles City, Montana, near where Calamity worked laying track and doing other odd jobs. MONTANA HISTORICAL SOCIETY RESEARCH CENTER PHOTOGRAPH ARCHIVES, HELENA, MT

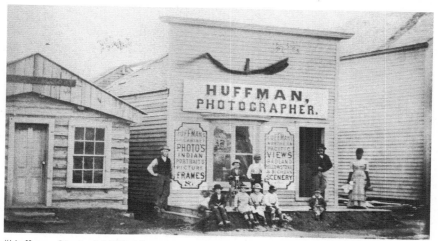

"Huffman Studio," 1881. View of L. A. Huffman's frame and photo studio in Miles City, Montana. Signs on the building read "Huffman, Photographer," "Huffman's Fine Cabinet Photos, Indian Portraits, Picture Frames etc.," and "Huffman's Northern Pacific Views, Badland, Yellowstone & Bighorn Scenery." Calamity Jane posed for several photos there. MONTANA HISTORICAL SOCIETY RESEARCH CENTER PHOTOGRAPH ARCHIVES, HELENA, MT

"Bull train, Main and Park Streets," 1881. Oxen pulling wagons down Miles City, Montana, streets. Frame and brick buildings in the background include signs for the Commercial Hotel and other businesses. MONTANA HISTORICAL SOCIETY RESEARCH CENTER PHOTOGRAPH ARCHIVES, HELENA, MT

"The Cosmopolitan Theatre," 1883. The theatre stood at Sixth and Main in Miles City. Several buildings are visible, including the theatre, C. W. Savage & Sons, and J. Baskinski & Bros. Photo taken by L. A. Huffman. MONTANA HISTORICAL SOCIETY RESEARCH CENTER PHOTOGRAPH ARCHIVES, HELENA, MT

"Log Cabin," the first house in the community of Greybull, built by John Borner in 1886. COURTESY WYOMING STATE ARCHIVES

Martha Jane Cannary's brother-in-law, John Borner, married to Lena Cannary. COURTESY WYOMING STATE ARCHIVES

"Calamity Jane" posing with amateur photographer John B. Mayo at Wild Bill Hickok's gravesite while Mayo's assistant made the exposure. COURTESY SOUTH DAKOTA STATE HISTORICAL SOCIETY

"Calamity Jane," posing in her Sunday finery for a studio portrait. COURTESY SOUTH DAKOTA STATE HISTORICAL SOCIETY

Studio portrait of "Calamity Jane" in a dress. COURTESY WYOMING STATE ARCHIVES

"Calamity Jane" posing for a studio photograph in fringed buckskin with holstered pistol and rifle in hand. COURTESY SOUTH DAKOTA STATE HISTORICAL SOCIETY

The *Kalispell Bee* article about Kid Curry and Butch Cassidy being arrested. They were part of the Hole in the Wall Gang, with whom Elijah Cannary is thought to have ridden and worked as an outlaw for a short time. MONTANA HISTORICAL SOCIETY RESEARCH CENTER PHOTOGRAPH ARCHIVES, HELENA, MT

"Elijah Cannary," uncropped photo showing handwritten notations of Calamity's brother, Lige, serving penitentiary time in Wyoming. COURTESY WYOMING STATE ARCHIVES

"Mt. Moriah Cemetery." Calamity Jane's grave and tombstone are on the right, next to Wild Bill Hickok's burial plot on the left. COURTESY SOUTH DAKOTA STATE HISTORICAL SOCIETY

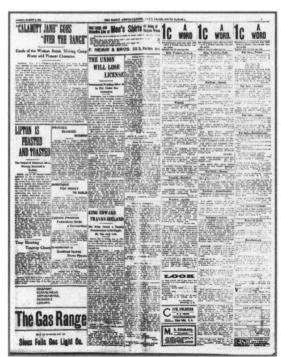

"Calamity Jane Obituary," Aug. 2, 1903. The obituary appeared on page 1 in the first column of the Sioux Falls, South Dakota, *Argus Leader*. COURTESY SOUTH DAKOTA STATE HISTORICAL SOCIETY

Chapter Eight

The Borners: Passing in Time

Jane has one recommendation, and that counts for considerable. She is perfectly willing to be what she seems to be and seem what she is.
—*St. Paul Dispatch*, July 13, 1901

After Lena's death in October 1888, John was heartbroken. He was also tired of battling his neighbors over water rights, so he sold his land near Lander to the State Poor Farm in 1888/89. That spring, he loaded his seven children into one covered wagon and his household belongings in another and set off for the family's new home in the Big Horn Basin. Trailing behind were a hundred head of cattle and twenty horses.

They arrived on May 16 just in time for a huge spring blizzard. The log cabin that he had built the previous year was waiting for them. Borner had brought along enough lumber to finish the floor.

When the weather had finally warmed enough to work outdoors, Borner went about clearing ten acres for farming and dug a cellar lined with lime rock as protection against Indian raids. Inside was an ample stockpile of food and fresh water—just in case. He instructed his children to stay in the cellar whenever he went to Billings for supplies, which was usually twice a year. He was usually gone for several weeks, so naturally the children failed to heed his instructions. As soon as he left, they popped out of the underground hideaway.

A daughter, Bertha Pauline, was seven at the time of the move and remembered the trip. The four mules that pulled the wagon didn't need any driving, she recalled, so the children sat in the wagon with a box of crackers and a jug of syrup. They dipped the crackers and ate their way to their new home. As might be expected, they "were smeared from one end to the other" by the time they arrived.

Credited for establishing the town of Lander, Borner had also become Greybull's first resident when he and his hired helper, J. A. Benjamin, built his new cabin on what would later become Greybull's City Park. Borner homesteaded all the land where the main part of the town lies today.

Once he and his children settled into their new home, Borner hired J. L. Denney to homeschool his children for three months while he worked setting up a water-delivery system similar to the one he had built on his ranch in Lander. He met with limited success until, in 1893, he managed to establish a ditch that tapped into the waters of Dry Creek. The name was indicative of the creek's reliability.

Although Borner chose not to remarry, he never allowed the lack of female companionship to prevent him from doing a good job raising the kids. Still, the Borner family did not skate through life without its share of problems. Before long, John realized that Calamity and Elijah weren't the only hell-raisers around. In 1900 alarming headlines appeared in the newspapers concerning Borner's son, Tobias, who ran afoul of the Alderdice boys, in-laws of the Borners. As a local paper reported, John and Albert Herbert Alderdice engaged Tobias "in a shooting affray in the mountains near Otto, Wyoming last Thursday. Three horses were killed and the Alderdice brothers, were seriously wounded. John received a ball in each arm and Albert [Herbert] was shot in the stomach. It is alleged that the two families have been at war for some time and further trouble will probably ensue."

The boys' father, Samuel Herbert Alderdice, had wed Tobias's sister, Hannah, in Casper, Wyoming, on March 17, 1900; but in this case, blood was hardly thicker than water. The Alderdice family had been among the first in the Greybull area and may have resented Borner's stature as the town's founding father. But whatever the reason for the fray, the *Sheridan Post* reported that there had been "bad blood" between the three boys for some time. It was no surprise that serious trouble erupted. After a chance meeting on the road, the Alderdice boys began shooting at Tobe Borner, whose team bolted and began to run.

> *By the time Borner succeeded in stopping his team, the other boys were out of ammunition and did not want to continue the fight. Borner then commenced to shoot and kill one horse and wound the other and shot John Alderdice through both arms, the ball entering the right arm and passing out through the left arm. Further trouble is now looked for between those parties.*

The *Post's* prophecy came true the following year. "Duelists Held for Trial" read the paper's horrifying headline.

> *Tobias Borner has been arrested on the charge of assault with intent to kill, and at his preliminary hearing was bound over to the district court. The complaining witnesses are Herbert and John Alderdice. The three men met on the train near Basin one day in January and fought a duel. The Alderdice brothers were wounded and Borner escaped unhurt.*

Upon Tobias's death of natural causes on July 13, 1950, at the age of seventy-three, the press remembered him not so much as the son of town founder John Borner but as the nephew of the notorious Calamity Jane. If Tobe had made contact with his famous kin in his later life, Calamity never revealed it. Still, since Tobias had begun freighting between Billings, Montana, and Lander, Wyoming, at the age of twenty, it's possible he ran into her on one of his numerous trips. Later, he moved to Shell, Wyoming, where he was connected with the Shell Creek Cattle Association. He was also once employed by the government as a forest ranger and hunter. In addition, Tobias wrote pioneer stories for the *Thermopolis Independent* newspaper. His byline was "Tobe Borner, Pioneer Cowboy." He died in a Billings, Montana, hospital as the result of a stroke suffered on the Fourth of July.

During the early 1900s John Borner's name began generating news for reasons other than his family's misadventures. He had connections to the Grand Army of the Republic (GAR) and had been a Mason in Utah before he ever stepped foot on Wyoming soil. He was prominent in Masonic affairs and was Master of Temple Lodge No. 20, A.F. and A.M. (Ancient Free and Accepted Masons) of Basin, Utah, in 1906/7. Always community-minded, he joined the County Fair Association in 1906 and became the post chaplain three years later.

John turned eighty in 1915, but he continued his service to the GAR and helped organize Memorial Day celebrations, which were always well attended. The newspaper reported, "A large crowd present to do honor to the old soldiers living and their comrades whose graves are found on countless hills and in as many dales. The exercises were enjoyed by all present, an excellent program having been prepared by the members of the G.A.R. These exercises were conducted by Commander John Borner."

When Borner died on December 13, 1919, of cerebral hemorrhage, he had the distinction of being the oldest Mason in the state, having been a member for fifty-nine years. The newspaper wrote a flowery obituary befitting the civil-mindedness of Greybull's first and finest citizen, Uncle Johnny Borner.

A lull of quiet came over the usually busy and noisy bustle of Greybull Avenue Thursday afternoon, as the members of the Masonic Lodge No. 34 of this city stood with bared heads in two lines, while the remains of John G. Borner were placed in the hearse at Cassel's undertaking parlors, from which place the Masons marched in body to the Baptist church, where services were conducted by Rev. Dean Watkins of the Episcopal church at Basin. Mr. Borner passed to the great beyond last Saturday, at the ripe old age of 84 years, 11 months and 9 days. Since the first days of our city he has been one of its best citizens, honest, industrious, faithful, and generous. He was even here before a city was ever platted, and homesteaded the land on which our flourishing city now stands. His homestead shack which he originally lived in still stands down by the Big Horn river, built after the style of most homestead shacks in the pioneer days of Wyoming, of logs. Coming here in early days, he lived to see Greybull's level, expanse transform from a stretch of sage brush into one of the liveliest cities of the state.

Borner was survived by his seven children and thirty-nine grandchildren upon his interment at the Greybull Cemetery.

Chapter Nine

Brother Lige

Lige would jump onto . . . [a] horse's back from the top rail of the fence and stay on as long as he could." Within three months of moving in with the Borners, he "had taught all the horses to buck, and since [John] Borner was no bronco buster, he didn't appreciate it.

—Tobe Borner

As with much of Calamity's life, details of her brother Elijah's time on earth both before and after living with the Borners are something of a mystery. But snapshots of facts gathered from newspaper clippings, legal documents, people's reminiscences, and other sources paint something of a portrait as to where and how he existed. It is not a pretty picture.

Most likely, Lige lived for some time with John and Lena in Lander following his return from the Black Hills Jenney Expedition with his sister Martha Jane. Just how long he lived with the newlyweds is unclear, although he may have worked in the laundry business Borner had established in a log cabin between Second and Third Streets for a while. Originally, Lena and Martha were slated to run the business, with Lige pitching in as his time and duties at the ranch allowed. But after only a few weeks, sister Calamity, predictably, became too busy chasing her own image to settle down and help run a business for any prolonged period of time.

Unfortunately, Tobe Borner never said how long Elijah worked for his brother-in-law. He never said what he did or where he went after leaving the Borner family, either, or if the family was on good terms when he parted. But, according to the 1880 census, Lige was no longer recorded as living with Lena, John, or their children, Mabel, Tobias, and Francis. That means that, like his older sis, he was on his own from a very young age.

In some ways, Elijah held the most promise of all the Cannary children. When he was young, he had Martha looking after him. As he grew older, he had Lena steering him right. When he moved in with the Borners following John and Lena's marriage, he must have felt as if he'd landed in heaven. Where else could he get a roof over his head, three meals a day, and unconditional love and nurturing—and still be able to work the horses he had come to love? They had become his passion and, in a way, his future downfall.

After leaving the Borner homestead for good, Lige rode the range roughshod across the plains and over the mountains of Utah, Idaho, and Wyoming. The 1880s proved to be a tumultuous time in the West, a time when the mountain states were plagued by outlaws, thieves, and murderers. Lige was none of those—at first. But from the late 1880s on into the new century, he became a sore on the backside of every lawman in the West. The rough-and-tumble boy he'd grown up to be while working on the ranch for his sister and brother-in-law remained part of who he would be for the rest of his life.

No doubt being orphaned so early left a mark on him. Primarily uneducated, opportunities for work and advancement proved scarce. Those jobs that did make themselves available were quickly filled by some of the dozens or even hundreds of transients wandering from one town to another.

Then, too, Elijah was no doubt influenced by his "wild cat" sister, Calamity Jane. After bonding with her on their journey together during the Black Hills expedition, he must have come to the conclusion that, if his sister could do something, he could, too. Ride, shoot, curse, spit, gamble, dance, get drunk, break the law, go to jail, get out, leave town—and then start all over again someplace new. All must have seemed to him to be a perfectly logical way of working one's way through life.

While Lige remained something of an enigma for much of his early years, his later "career" kept the newspapermen wagging their tongues. The Fourth Estate in the West back then was little more than a gossip mill at any rate; but when a story of potential prominence presented itself, the reporters rarely let it pass unnoticed—whether or not it was true.

One correspondent who went by the name of MyFanwy Thomas Goodnough reported in a November 2, 1893, issue of the *Wyoming State Tribune* that two of Calamity Jane's brothers lived in the Star Valley in the village of Freedom. Elijah may have been one of them, but the only other brother Calamity had was Cilus, who had died when he was a small boy. Still, even though the details of the story were askew, the Teton Basin to the north of Star Valley would turn out to play a prominent role in Lige's life.

In 1879 The Church of Jesus Christ of Latter-day Saints (LDS)—the Mormons—settled in an area that came to be known as a haven for polygamists, a practice that was frowned upon by most U.S. citizens and many states. The Mormons named the town they founded Freedom for apparent reasons. Set on the border between Wyoming and Idaho, the town's main street running north and south straddled the state line, enabling fugitives from justice to enjoy the ability to escape the long arm of the law with impunity. When a Wyoming police officer appeared in town, the bad guys simply stepped across the street into Idaho. When the Idaho law showed up with their warrants, the criminals stepped back across the street into Wyoming. It was a quick, easy, and effective means of avoiding apprehension—at least for a while.

When the U.S. Congress outlawed polygamy in 1887, the Star Valley Mormons, who had vowed to continue the practice, found themselves out of the limelight and out of the law's hair—which is exactly how they wanted things. Likewise, fugitive outlaws who used the entire region of Star Valley as a hideout operated openly with impunity. On the way to nowhere special and leading back from nowhere in particular, the Teton Basin was tucked away into the mountains and shrouded in snow for more than half the year. It was the perfect hideaway.

Elijah's settling in the Star Valley area may have been coincidence, but more likely it was an indication that he was already deeply involved in illegal activities. He went there to hide out. Alone? That's doubtful, since the area was a refuge for outlaws such as Butch Cassidy, the Sundance Kid, Mat Warner, Bub Meeks, and others. Melding in with the bandits, miners, polygamists, and those simply tired of life in the fast lane, they made themselves at home, participating in community affairs and, for the most part, minding their manners.

At the town's Auburn Church, they indulged in the social and religious activities, and whenever a dance was held there, they were among the first to attend, as reporter Lee R. Call noted in the *Star Valley Independent*:

> *The dance hall was usually so crowded the dance tickets were numbered and just one third of those attending could dance at a time. Some of the young men bought a number of tickets so they could get in more dances.*

If the Goodnough newspaper article is correct and Elijah lived in Freedom, he probably had connections with outlaws who lived in the valley—perhaps even Cassidy's Wild Bunch. Elijah could even have attended the dances at the Auburn church and learned a tip or two about the bad guys' horse-stealing activities, which were widespread throughout the 1800s. At one point in his life, Elijah, too, was enticed by the prospect of easy money. An 1885 issue of the *Uinta Chieftain* reprinted a plea for help originally printed in the *Cheyenne Tribune:*

> *Would it not be well for the authorities of the United States and of the territory to give a little more attention to the life and property of bona fide residents from the operations of murderers and thieves. Reports come daily of depredations of outlaws in the northwestern portion of the territory. Late reports from the northwestern portion of the Teton country, places the number of horse thieves and desperadoes who make that region their head quarters at from sixty or seventy.*

One of the most perfect examples of a protected hideout for outlaws lay deep within the Teton Basin, surrounded by the Rocky Mountains. With its single pass in and single pass out, it provided a nearly impregnable refuge, especially during the winter months when the passes filled with deep snow, blanketing the inhabitants in pristine white seclusion. Once ensconced in their sturdy log cabins, the bandits found their fortresses "could be held against almost anything, but artillery."

The basin, still remote and wild to this day, extended for nearly twenty square miles. That made easy going for the horse thieves in the area who herded their stolen animals into the secluded canyon. The well-watered rich bunch grass provided necessary nourishment to fatten the horses during the winter months, when the bandits curtailed their raids. When the last of the stolen horses was herded into the valley, the brands were reworked by "applying the red bottom of a frying pan to the brands necessary to be obliterated." The bandits covered the burned area with grease, which caused the hair to grow back by spring, disguising any trace of the original brand. Afterwards, the outlaws used a branding iron to place new markings on the animal to make it look as if it belonged to them. Proving otherwise was nearly impossible, as an article in the *Laramie Daily Boomerang* described.

After the job was done, the bandits hunted, gambled and drank whiskey, joined in shooting matches and horse racing to pass the winter days. In May the horses were rounded up, divided up into small bands, sleek and fat, and then were taken slowly in different directions to various points and disposed of.

Not surprisingly, gangs of horse thieves terrorized the bi-state area, stealing the best horses from Idaho and Wyoming before selling them the following spring, being cautious not to offer the stock back to the same ranchers from whom they had stolen them. Sometimes, they drove the horses as far away as Montana and Dakota Territory to sell.

The plan worked well—nearly too well. Most likely Elijah stumbled across the scheme and, already on the run for minor legal infringements, hooked up with the thieves. And he enjoyed quite a bit of success. But not all was sweetness and light for Calamity's baby brother. In time, Elijah was arrested on charges of horse stealing and brought to trial. On June 15, 1894, prosecuting attorney John C. Hamm, representing the State of Wyoming, County of Uinta, informed the court that "Cannary a fugitive from Justice . . . unlawfully, feloniously, willfully and maliciously on the track of the Oregon Short Line Railroad in said county, by placing thereon horses and livestock, did place obstructions so as to endanger the passing of trains thereon." The attorney also implicated Lige's partner, Oliff Hclquist, alias J. B. Johnson, with the same crime.

The railroad that the prosecutor referred to was the Oregon Short Line, which Elijah and his accomplices had targeted for their scheme. It was a subsidiary of the Union Pacific Railroad, providing a shorter route from Wyoming to Oregon.

As Lige and his partner laid out their planned attacks against the railroad, they were confident. They had a nearly foolproof plan that had worked several times in the past.

But this time was different. Although their crime went off without a hitch, someone snitched, and a warrant was soon issued for Elijah's arrest.

Elijah was no one if not a dreamer. Like his sister before him, he had determined that the best way out of his dead-end life was to invent a totally different one. So he began plying his charms on an innocent, young, impressionable girl and her family, somehow managing to hide his checkered past from them. For Lige, the young girl and her family meant a life and future that he had always dreamt of—and expected would come his way. When his mother and father had died—and his sister Martha Jane left him in an orphanage in Salt Lake City—he began to realize that, if his life was ever going to change, he would need to be the one to change it.

So he soon began courting Kate E. Carson in Ogden, Utah. Before long, he asked for her hand, and she agreed. Finally, on November 17, 1895, the local newspaper printed a notice: "Late Saturday a marriage license was issued to Eliza [Elijah] Canary, aged 28, and Kate E. Carson, aged 16, both of Ogden. Rev. T. L. Crandall of the Baptist church last night performed the ceremony uniting them in marriage." Kate's sister, Mollie, fourteen, and Edward Pearce were their witnesses. "The wedding was very quiet owing to the illness of the bride's mother," the article continued, never once speculating that the mother's illness might have been brought by her daughter's sudden marriage!

While the ceremony had been fairly ordinary, Kate wasn't. She had come from an extraordinary family. Katherine Exarmina Carson was the eldest daughter of Frank and Irene Carson's prominent Mormon family in Ogden, Utah. Her father had come from Louisville, Kentucky. He traveled extensively as a child, and on his return from Australia to New Orleans, he found himself in the middle of the Civil War. He immediately joined the Confederacy, where he attained the rank of captain before the war ended and he was mustered out.

Following the fighting, he caught a wagon train west, and when it stopped in Colorado, he jumped off, rented a room, and found employment driving stagecoaches for the Ben Holiday Line from Denver to Cheyenne and back. While in Colorado, he married Irene Jane Carroll at Fort Collins in 1869. Shortly after the nuptials were completed, Frank became a surveyor for the railroad. He was behind a surveyor's glass when gold was discovered at Cripple Creek, Colorado, in 1883. A short time later he moved with his wife to the Mormon community of Ogden, where Frank and his new wife became active in civic and community affairs. When he finally passed away in 1908, his obituary opined:

Frank Carson, one of the oldest and best-known residents of Ogden, died this morning at 8 o'clock, at his residence, 2259 Read Avenue. Death resulted from a complication of liver complaint and tuberculosis.

The deceased was born in Louisville, Kentucky, May 9, 1840, and participated in the war of the Rebellion as a captain of the famous Louisiana Tigers on the Confederate side. He was one of the early "whips" on the overland stage route and on two different occasions had his stage robbed of its horses by Indians. He was a second cousin of the famous Kit Carson, had traveled extensively in all parts of the world, and leaves a host of friends from California to the Missouri river to mourn his loss and revere his memory. The funeral will be held from the residence at 3 p.m., Sunday, members of the local G.A.R. attending by reason of a request he made just before dying.

A different headline in a competing paper shouted, "Kit Carson's Cousin Dies in Ogden." Yet another obituary claimed that Frank had been personally acquainted with western folk heroes such as California Joe, Buffalo Bill Cody, and Wild Bill Hickok, among others.

Frank's wife, not to be outdone, boasted her own credentials. Irene Carson had born and raised nine children, including two sets of twins, and was actively involved in the Ladies of the Maccabees, the Silver Hive No. 1, where she served in several offices, one of which was as Lady Commander.

While some people question just how much of a stir an outlaw in their midst might have affected the Carson family clan, it's notable that a large number of outlaws were scattered throughout the West. You could hardly throw a stick without hitting one—and presumably suffering the consequences! So, following their marriage, Lige and Kate retired to their new home. But their joy wasn't to last long.

On December 3, 1895, less than a month after the wedding, a criminal warrant from Uinta County was issued for Lige's arrest. He was charged with the crime of placing obstructions on the railroad tracks. More specifically, placing *horses* on the tracks. A warrant was issued at the same time for Oliff Helquist (Hilquist), alias J. B. Johnson, and William Dawling, alias William Kunz, the same day.

Where it was that Elijah was arrested remains a mystery. The *Ogden Standard* headlined a special news story, claiming, "An Important Arrest, Elijah Cannary an Alleged Wyoming Criminal Jailed Here Saturday." The story claimed that Sheriff Wright had arrested Elijah in Ogden at Landsberg's Saloon. He said that Cannary was wanted in Idaho and Wyoming on several different charges involving horse theft. The paper reported that Elijah was one of the ringleaders of an organized gang of outlaws that, for several years, had been operating in Wyoming and Idaho. Their crime: horse theft and bribery. Wrote another local paper:

It is said that their method has been to steal horses. . . . This nefarious scheme is said to have been worked very successfully and the gang has obtained several hundred dollars through the courts in this way. It is said that another of the ring leaders of the gang is now in jail in Evanston and others are being arrested on suspicion of being implicated in the work of the criminals.

Several other newspapers carried the charge that the notorious horse thieves operating in the area had been arrested. A January article in a Laramie newspaper said, "Lige Cannary has been arrested in Uinta County charged with herding his horses on the railroad track at night for the purpose of having the cars kill them so that he could secure damages from the railroad company." An Idaho newspaper reported that the thieves were finally apprehended after a long and harrowing chase. He and Will Kunz were arrested on the charge of "driving stock onto the track in Wyoming for the purpose of filching dollars from the Union Pacific." Several months later, on April 14, 1896, Kunz was also arrested and thrown in the county jail to await trial.

Duncan McLennan, a businessman and long-time Kunz family acquaintance from Cokerville, Wyoming, wrote to Judge Jesse Knight that Kunz was an outstanding citizen and was obviously influenced by others. McLennan vouched for the Kunz family, insisting it was highly regarded within the community. He asked for leniency in passing sentence, reminding the court that Kunz's wife and family were dependent on him for their existence. McLennan concluded that "this will be a good lesson to him."

Several months after the marriage between Elijah and Kate, the April 22, 1896, issue of the *Wind River Mountaineer* reported that Elijah Cannary and William Kunz had pled guilty to the "charge of driving horses upon the intention of having them killed by trains and thereafter demanding remuneration from the railroad company." The article mentioned that "Canary is a brother of the famous Calamity Jane." It was one of the first times a newspaper had connected Calamity and Elijah in print.

Following a lengthy trial, Lige and his cohorts were convicted and sent to the Wyoming territorial penitentiary in Laramie. The *Statesman* wrote that, while others were involved in the gang, the investigating officers were unable to locate them. Finally, a confession was secured from one of the Wyoming convicts implicating Helquist. Unfortunately, Helquist was already an inmate of the Idaho penitentiary, so "A requisition for his extradition to Wyoming was issued yesterday," the article said.

Meanwhile, Sheriff Ward delivered the convicts to the Laramie warden. Judge Knight sentenced William Kunz to seven years for obstructing railroads and Elijah Canary to five years for the same crime.

It was time then for Officer Joe Jones from Bear Lake County to arrest Oliff Helquist the moment he stepped from the Idaho penitentiary, where he had been incarcerated for the prior year for grand larceny committed in Bingham County. The newspaper termed the charge against Helquist *peculiar*.

"Helquist," the paper reported, "was one of a gang that for some time bled the Union Pacific in Idaho and Wyoming." The article explained:

The plan of the crowd was to run a herd of stolen stock onto the railroad track and keep them there until a train came along during the night and tore some of them into mince meat. A claim for damages would then be filed and, after the usual red-tape process, a compromise would be affected, whatever the gang received being clear profit. The frequency with which claims came in from first one and then the other of the gang aroused the suspicions of the Union Pacific officers and detectives were placed on their trail.

By September 12, 1896, Helquist, who admitted to being a laborer by profession, was incarcerated in the county jail. The stay didn't last long. The twenty-nine-year-old Helquist was sentenced on September 26, 1896, to serve a two-year term and discharged on June 17, 1898, without pardon.

Not coincidentally, both of Elijah's accomplices, Helquist and Kunz, were Mormons from Montpelier, Idaho. The town had been founded by the Mormons and named by their spiritual leader, Brigham Young. Since

Elijah lived and even worked in the area, he had most likely met the two men there. In fact, since Lige had spent much of his youth among the Mormons, it's likely he felt most comfortable among members of the LDS church. In fact, he even claimed to be Mormon at one point in his life, while at another time he insisted he'd had little or no religious training, Mormon or otherwise.

In July 1897, after serving some of his prison sentence, William Kunz applied for a pardon on the grounds that his wife and two children were destitute. The Idaho sheriff and the Oregon Short Line railroad blocked the pardon; but Wyoming governor William Richards, who was criticized for the number of pardons he routinely granted, commuted the seven-year sentence. Kunz walked out of prison on January 24, 1899, nearly two years earlier than would Elijah.

Not surprisingly, Elijah's young wife took her husband's criminal conviction hard. Kate was an impressionable young lady who was expecting the couple's first child. She apparently held no hard feelings against her husband, for when the child was born, she named him Frank Elijah.

When Kate and her family learned of Kunz's early release, they hired attorneys Allen & Allen of San Francisco to plead to Governor Richards for executive clemency for Lige. The Carson family apparently believed Elijah was a victim of circumstances—someone in the wrong place at the wrong time. No one believed he was an unreformed criminal. Or so it appeared.

In a long rambling letter to the governor, the Carson attorneys pointed out that Elijah Cannary had been employed by Kuntz (Kunz) and was simply following orders. Furthermore, the attorneys insisted that "but a short time prior to his imprisonment the said Canary was married and his wife and child are now suffering for the necessaries of life and are dependent upon the said Canary for support."

The attorneys went on to write:

Mr. Canary's wife and her family desire the pardon of her husband. First:—Upon the ground that he was not interested or connected with the crime except as a hired servant. . . . Second:—He has served almost three (3) years of his sentence and was the willing witness for the State to bring the guilty leader to justice. Third:—He was never charged of crime before and has not since conducted himself as a willful criminal. Fourth:—His wife and family guarantee to bring him to California where he can support and care for them. Fifth:—The ends of justice have been fully compensated by his imprisonment. Sixth:— Executive clemency is the only hope of relief in such cases.

On August 12, 1900, six months after the Carson family's plea for early release, Elijah was paroled for good conduct, shortening his original sentence of five years by slightly more than eight months. According to the 1900 census, Kate and son, Frank, who had just turned three, were living with Kate's parents and family in Ogden. The census recorded Kate as being divorced. She and her sister Mollie were working as sales ladies to help support their twelve-member household. Ironically, after all her family had done to help secure Lige's release, when he walked out of prison, he was a divorced man. Kate had simply given up on him—or perhaps her family had persuaded her he would never amount to anything.

But Elijah Cannary couldn't have disagreed more. Filled with the hopes and dreams and ambitions of his Big Sis, he set out to prove to the world he was right. He just didn't yet know how, and he didn't know where.

Chapter Ten

The Taming of a Shrew

Over the years, Calamity claimed to have married about a dozen different men. At various times, in various places, she lived with soldiers, ranchers, and miners she called her husbands. But most of their names have long since been forgotten.
—Doris Faber, *Calamity Jane: Her Life and Her Legend*

Between 1888 and 1891, Calamity staggered from one Wyoming town to another. In the year 1889 alone she was reported being in Lander, Rock Springs, Green River, Cheyenne, the Newcastle area, and, that fall, in Casper. She may even have wandered down into the flatlands of Nebraska.

In July 1888, according to newspaper reports, Calamity was alleged to be in a bawdy house in Tubb Town, near Newcastle. If so, she must have been anything but the "hardened whore" of Western lore. One woman in Tubb Town observed Calamity enter a dry-goods store, "caress" a piece of fabric, and buy it, referring to it as "so sweet and girlish." Later, early in 1890, Calamity was off to Wendover and then Cheyenne. Before the end of the year, she was in Fort Washakie before traveling back to northeastern Wyoming.

Not too surprisingly, the details missing from reports of Calamity's frequent travels are as revealing as the published reports. One of these missing details concerned the state of Calamity's young daughter, Jessie.

Where was the girl staying, at age two or three, when Calamity spent the night on the town, or worse? With Lena gone and no other family to turn to, who took care of Jessie? It may have been the Steers family, some of whom lived in and around Lander, but accounts don't say. Neither did the records provide any mention of any specific jobs Calamity may have held during these years, except in the cat house in Tubb Town.

Most certainly, even if Steers's family did provide care and housing for the youngster, what would have happened to the girl once Steers left Calamity for good? Certainly, Calam was in no position to raise a daughter. When she found herself homeless and, once again, without a man in her life, she seemed to lose all semblance of order to her life. By the time she was in her mid-thirties, she was obviously having trouble staving off the effects of alcoholism and joblessness. To those who knew her best, she appeared to be on the verge of mental and physical collapse. Not at all a first for Ms. Martha Jane Cannary.

The unrecorded wanderings of the amazing plainswoman continued into the early 1890s, although we can guess that she took advantage of the new railroad lines opening up the West to explore new venues. Calamity may have bounced around Wyoming, stopping off at the mining boomtown of Creede, Colorado. She had been seen as far east as Omaha, Nebraska, telling a reporter she ran across that she was traveling to Iowa to visit relatives. In fact, by that time, she may have recognized that Lander held nothing more for her since her sister's death, and abandoned it to history. But later, in 1893, she was reportedly seen haunting the halls of Rawlins and Laramie in the company of a former "husband," Mr. King. Even more interestingly, she had in her company a small child—a girl child.

In time, Calamity moved north, driving bull teams in Sheridan. One tall tale had her drinking with Buffalo Bill there, although no histories of Cody—despite the fact that Jane knew him—confirm such an event.

After that, Calamity worked her way north through Wyoming, returning to the Billings area in 1893/94. Several reports place her there, commenting on her activities. Years later, Calamity's daughter, Jessie, recalled that she and her mother were in Billings by 1893. Others living near Billings at the time remembered hearing about a woman named Calamity. A young man living on a ranch outside of Billings talked about

Calamity hauling wood to town to sell to survive. He thought she also had worked cleaning hotel rooms and bars.

During the year that Calamity resided in a cabin outside of town, she was called upon to participate in the documentation of a historical event, one of the rare times in her life. The event resulted in a little-known photograph of her. It was during the Panic of 1893 that a gaggle of angry miners, upset with the struggling U.S. economy and a paucity of jobs, purloined a Northern Pacific train and drove it east to Billings, planning to join Coxey's Army in its famous march on Washington to protest. On the tracks near Billings in spring 1894, Calamity, the only woman in the bunch sent to stop them, stood with a dozen or two soldiers and other men and boys, guarding the engine against further attempts at a takeover by the miners.

Despite this and a few other reported incidents, Calamity's life seemed relatively ordered and calm in 1893/94, compared to the frenetic and aimless wandering of the previous several years. She must have hoped to provide some balance of home and family life for Jessie, who was with her at the time in Billings. Perhaps, too, a new male companion furnished new balance to Calamity's oft-precarious life.

Sometime in the early 1890s, Calamity met a young man by the name of Clinton E. Burke. After a whirlwind "courtship," he became her "husband" and remained such for the next three or four years. Much of the populist press of the time ate that story up, reveling in the fact that the incorrigible Ms. Martha Jane had finally had the wind stolen from her sails and settled down to normalcy on the open prairies outside of El Paso, Texas. Nothing could have been further from the truth.

Clinton E. Burke had been born in Saline County, Missouri, in 1867, the son of a Presbyterian minister. His father died in 1887, which may have been the reason for young Clint (sometimes known as Charley) heading west. In eastern Montana, Burke met a young man who regaled him with tales of the exploits of a gal named Calamity Jane in the Black Hills.

Burke looked him in the eye and told him he knew all about her: "She's my wife."

Calamity and Burke remained together until 1896 or slightly later. Burke was considerably younger than Calamity, as were Bill Steers before him and Robert Dorsett after him. Still, despite whatever efforts Calamity put into settling down for good, doing so was simply not in her nature. By summer of 1894, she had moved with Burke back to Miles City, Montana, where they lived in a tumbledown abandoned shack behind the Grey Mule Saloon. Near her stood the Hi Astle stable where she met one-time cowboy W. H. (Wirt) Newcom. She told Newcom that she had married a "fellow by the name of Burke." After introducing her husband to him, Newcom said he thought she'd made a "handsome" choice, just as she had with Wild Bill. Martha agreed, saying, "I never had a fellow with a h*** of a lot of money; I always did pick a good looker."

The two men hit it off and, together with Calamity, became good friends.

Unfortunately, Calamity got in trouble one night and was arrested—most likely for rowdiness. When the sheriff released her so that she could go scrape up the bail, she made a beeline for the livery stable where she woke Newcom, telling him that she needed him to take her to Deadwood. "Ed Jackson put me in jail because I was a celebrity," she said, "and Judge Milburn fined me one hundred dollars. I haven't got any money." Martha told him she intended "to make a run for it," Newcom added.

But Newcom was alone in the stable, so he couldn't leave town. But he managed to dig up a cowpuncher who agreed to help. When her rescuers stopped by her house, "Jane came out with her war bag and we carried out a cheap suitcase, and all that was good old Jane's 'forty year's' gatherings."

When Martha stopped to bid Newcom good-bye, she said, "You tell old Jackson . . . Slim, he ought to be ashamed of himself. Do you know it took him and two more men to put me in jail? Tell him for me some day I am coming back here to Miles City and I will whip h*ll out of him." With that, she bid him good-bye, and Newcom wished her the best.

But Martha never made it to Deadwood—at least not that night. She next popped up with Burke in Ekalaka, Montana, better known as Pup Town, a small cow town in the southeastern corner of the state some twenty-five miles from the South Dakota border. There they lived as a family in a tent half a mile from Cap Harmon's sprawling "22 Ranch," where her husband worked in 1894/95. Harmon's son, Dick, remembered that Martha "was married to one of our cowboys—Jack Burke [*sic*]. She had a little girl she said was her daughter with her." Another Ekalaka resident, Ida Castleberry, also recalled Martha, Burke, along with "their daughter, a little girl about five, six or seven years old." They "lived in a tent," Castleberry said, adding that "Calamity took care of a sick woman for a few days," making her "well liked."

Sixty years later, Dick Harmon could still recall Calamity's stay in the area. "Jane wore overalls and dressed just like a man. She would often engage in wrestling matches with Jack [Clinton] and she often won. . . . She smoked and chewed and was almost as profane as her husband, who swore and cursed in a loud voice at the horses he was plowing with." Calamity was similarly adept at "borrowing" milk from the cows until Clinton was relieved of that chore. After Calamity and Burke left the ranch, young Harmon, while riding near their tent site, discovered a hole overflowing with chicken heads and feathers, solving the mystery of where so many of the ranch's missing fowl had gone.

With wanderlust once more getting the best of Jane, she headed back to the Black Hills, which was but a short jaunt from Ekalaka. Perhaps Calam, having seen the possibilities lying before her as a Wild West performer in the Coeur d'Alenes and with Hardwick in the mid-1880s, hungered for some of the excitement and publicity awaiting her as a Wild West show performer. So in 1895 Martha Jane finally made it back to Deadwood. It was her first time there since 1879. To say that the locals were happy to see her might well be the understatement of the century. The *Black Hills Daily Times* reported on October 5, 1895, that "'Calamity Jane!' The Fearless Indian Fighter and Rover of the Western Plains" was back in Deadwood. The return to the scene of her earliest notoriety would become a highlight of her final years on earth, a time during which most people of her stature would have taken comfort and solace and enjoyed every minute of the adulation she was destined to receive.

But that was for most people.

Calamity Jane was anything *but* most people.

CHAPTER ELEVEN

An Unanticipated Endorsement

Do you remember, Judge . . . the time Calamity pulled a gun and a volley of language on a bull-whacker down here because he was belaboring a tired ox? He didn't even [dare] frown at the beast when she got through with him.

—ESTELLINE BENNETT, *OLD DEADWOOD DAYS*

SIXTEEN LONG YEARS FOLLOWING CALAMITY'S LAST VISIT TO DEADwood had done nothing to dull her notoriety *or* her welcome. If anything, her absence had indeed made the residents' hearts grow fonder.

But this time, her fall 1895 visit brought with it one glaring difference. The October 5 edition of the *Black Hills Daily Times* declared, "Calamity Jane's in town." She had arrived only the day before. A driver at the railway station recounted picking up two passengers—one, "a short, heavy set, dark complexioned woman of about 43 years, clad in a plain black dress, and beside her sat a little girl who has seen probably nine summers."

Once word of Calam's arrival—and with a young girl, no less—spread through town, a crowd gathered to take in the sight. Calamity, never shy around people, took her daughter with her to the sheriff's office, where she agreed to a newspaper interview with a *Daily Times* reporter. As well-wishers and gawkers alike swelled the room, she told her audience that she and her husband, Burke (who was to join her shortly), had been living with their daughter on a ranch not far outside Ekalaka. But she never really liked "that kind of life" and decided to return to Deadwood. There she hoped she'd find "some respectable employment that . . . [would] afford herself and the little girl a living and give her child the benefit of the schools."

Calamity also shared a few ideas about her thoughts and plans for the future. Since she disliked "newspaper notoriety" because so many reporters had lied about her in the past, she eschewed sharing more information about her life with them. Also, although she was told she "could make lots of money by traveling with some good show," she didn't cater much to that idea, either. They were two simple statements that, on the surface, sounded perfectly logical.

Except that there was precious little that Calam did or said that proved to be logical. The *Times* reporter quoted Calamity as stating that no "authentic" account of her life had ever been written, so "she thought that she would narrate the numerous incidents . . . to some good writer sometime and have it published." In fact, she had already arranged to do so; and some of the interview she granted ended up being transcribed into her autobiography, published later that year.

And far from eschewing the notion of traveling around the country in a Wild West show somewhere, she had already contracted with one tour group to do just that, although she had squandered that opportunity by failing to keep an appointment with them earlier that year. So, while Calamity was telling the reporter about how she hoped to find gainful employment in the Deadwood area while placing her daughter in a suitable school, she was, in fact, already thinking seriously about hitting the trail once more, this time as a Wild Western performer.

A woman named Estelline Bennett wrote thirty years later of Calamity's return to Deadwood in her book, *Old Deadwood Days* (1928). The daughter of the only federal judge in the Deadwood area, Bennett was in her late twenties in the 1890s. As part of Deadwood's honored "elite," it surprised people to see her paint a much more sympathetic portrait of Calamity than Martha had read in most other Dakota and Montana newspapers. Bennett didn't disagree with the *Times* reporter in recounting Calamity as "dressed in shabby clothes" and "leading her little seven-year-old girl by the hand." The *Times's* description of her dress as being a "dark cloth coat . . . never had been good, a cheap little hat, a faded frayed shirt, and arctic overshoes" caught Bennett's attention right off. Calamity had revealed to Bennett that she had donated her shoes to a woman whose own shoes wouldn't have lasted another brutal South Dakota winter. That left Calamity with nothing to wear on her feet but her over-boots.

Bennett also noted that, despite her notoriety, Calamity Jane's Deadwood lay a generation in the past. Quite a bit of water had flowed under the bridge since the famed plainswoman had last visited there when Calamity and Wild Bill took the town by storm. In the interim, Deadwood had grown. It was no longer the mining boomtown of 1876. It was more cosmopolitan, more diverse upon Calamity's second time through. And she was no longer emblematic of the new Deadwood but, rather, a symbol of the Deadwood of the past that had by then been so long gone. Perhaps it was that realization that spurred her on to believing that she, too—like the town she had once stormed—had a future in the reconstruction of the history of the Old West.

Within a day or two of arriving in Deadwood, Calamity moved to the nearby town of Lead with predictable results. The *Lead Evening Call* reported that, upon her mere presence, "a large crowd soon gathered on the opposite corner of the bank to catch sight of this much-noted woman." As had happened in Deadwood, old-timers in Lead welcomed Calamity as a returning celebrity. But when she appeared in town, she had "a fair sized jag [drunk] on board, and this, together with a reprehensible cigar she smoked, made her look anything but the beautiful woman that the dime novelists and storytellers had written about so much." In reality, Calamity was so drunk that she "had to be assisted into a hack" by an officer, "to whom she used vile language." Not long after, the sheriff "invited" her to leave town.

Returning once more to Deadwood, Calamity found that her reputation—the *real* one she had developed for drinking, whoring, and catting around—had preceded her. Some people, particularly those who had never known her in the "good old days," took to railing against her very presence. But others showed less animosity and more sympathy. Realizing how serious Calamity's need to educate her daughter, Jessie, was, several Deadwood residents threw a fund-raising evening for

Calamity at the Green Front, a slaughterhouse of a saloon in one of the seediest parts of town. By the time the funds had been counted, Calamity had already gone through half the donations by setting up free drinks for the sponsors. Fortunately, she couldn't spend it all fast enough, and some funds remained for their intended use.

Not about to be outdone by its sister city to the east, the residents of Lead announced a "Bloomer Ball" to be held in Calamity's support. The masquerade was meant "as a benefit for the noted Jane," who had been observed trying to raise money for her support by selling her photographs on the street. But the night of the ball proved disappointing when the guest of honor failed to show up. As one reporter phrased it, the "grand old ruin [Calamity] was in temporary retirement at Hot Springs, so her presence was necessarily dispensed with."

As the year slowly ground to an end, Calamity continued circulating among the towns and camps of the Black Hills, selling her photographs to anyone who would buy. The local newspapers, once friendly to her exploits, began swinging their sentiments against her. They called her out for her reckless drinking and "obscene" acts. Calamity, true to form, denied everything, pointing out that she had never abused women or done any of the other things the papers alleged. To prove it—and perhaps to salvage what remained of a tarnished reputation—she enrolled her daughter in Deadwood's St. Edwards Academy. But the arrangement soon soured, and Calamity was forced to remove her, enrolling her in St. Martin's Academy in Sturgis. That, too, soon turned ugly, for although the girl was receiving *some* education, she spent most of her time trying to sidestep the ridicule heaped upon her for being the daughter of "Calamity Jane." Jessie, an inordinately shy girl who felt out of place anywhere except at her mother's side, suffered the slings and arrows of her classmates, including the boys, who regularly threw stones at her in an attempt to run her off the school grounds.

Although Calamity said little about this time in her life, a female journalist in early 1896 asked for an interview. Calamity agreed, providing one of the most illuminating accounts of the Wild West figure ever recorded.

M. L. Fox caught up with the plainswoman when she was living with Clinton Burke and Jessie in Deadwood just as the family was making preparations to go on the road with the Kohl and Middleton traveling show. While the vast majority of newspaper articles written about Calamity came from male journalists (female reporters were something of a rarity), Fox was one of the few exceptions. And the article shows the differing approaches between her and other writers.

Instead of dwelling on Calamity's sensationalized western experiences, Fox dug into Martha's life as a wife and mother. Perhaps surprisingly, Calamity revealed more in that single article than she had in all the press coverage before or after.

Fox began her article by setting the scene, beginning with Calamity's appearance and her surroundings. When the reporter appeared at California Jack's house, where Calamity was staying, she asked for the celebrity by name.

"That's me," came the response. "Walk right in. Rather dirty-lookin' house, but we've been 'bout sick an' let things go." Calamity expressed concern about her appearance, another rare confession: "I ain't combed my head to-day; looks like it, too, I 'spose."

Fox herself described Calamity as being "of medium height, robust, rather inclined to stoutness, and looks to be in the prime of life, but I believe she is past that, though her hair, which is long, still retains its natural brown color; her eyes are dark gray, and their expressions are many. Her chin is firm and mouth decided."

When Fox inquired about Calamity's personal history, she said she was "past forty-three: everybody says I don't look it, but it's 'cause I've lived outdoors so much an' had good health." [In reality, Calamity turned forty in 1896, although she often claimed a birth date of 1852—the same year as she credited in her autobiography, which was coincidentally published around the same time as Fox's interview.]

"I was born in Missouri," Calamity told the reporter, "but my folks moved to Montana when I was quite young. We lived all over the West, an' father and mother died when I was nine year ole." As an orphan, she recalled living "near a post, an' them soldiers took care of me. I didn't know nothing 'bout women ner how white folks lived; all I knowed was how to rustle grub an' steal rides behind the stage-coaches an' camp with the Injuns." Even though Calamity wanted to open up to the woman reporter, she couldn't help slipping back into some of the tall tales she had relayed for most of her life, including those she would include in her autobiography.

Fox went on to draw out the differences between Calamity Jane with her rough, unkempt appearance and crude language, and those of her "husband," Clinton Burke—and even her daughter, Jessie. "Mr. Burk [sic]," Fox wrote, was "a young-looking man, whose white linen and good clothes looked rather out of place in the room, that would have been quite home-like but for its disorder." Calamity went out of her way to convince Fox that, unlike with some of her "husbands," she was actually legally married to Burke, recounting that, "I'm honestly married to this man. I had to go to Texas to get him. . . . Nobody'd have me here."

She went on to describe her family as decent, hard-working folks who had lived on a ranch in Montana, worked in a nearby logging camp, and opened a business in a mining town. The business soon went broke, and Calamity confessed that "we lost everything."

Perhaps it was Calamity's unbridled sincerity than won Fox over. More likely it was observing firsthand the legend's attitude toward her daughter. As the interview was progressing, the door to the cabin squeaked open, and Jessie walked in from school. Fox observed her as being a "neatly-dressed girl . . . shy and embarrassed" of "about nine years of age." She wrote that the girl "had a bright face, and her manners were very good for one whose opportunities had been so few."

As Fox delved into Calamity's maternal side, wondering how Jane had managed to marry motherhood with the Wild West Legend, Calamity's face grew long, and tears formed in the corners of her eyes. "All I ask is to be spared an' have my health so's to give my little girl an education," she said, "so when I do go she will have some way to support herself if she don't get married. . . . I don't care what they say 'bout me, but I want my daughter to be honest an' respectable. . . . She's all I've got to live fer; she's my only comfort. I had a little boy but he died."

By then, Calamity's composure had abandoned her as she wept openly.

When, after calming her subject down, Fox asked if Calamity planned on staying in Deadwood, she replied, "We're [she and Burke] on our way East." She said she planned on leaving Jessie in a convent school and would take her chances with "shows an' the like in the East."

As the interview began winding down, Fox held out her hand to thank Calamity for her time. Calamity took hold of it, admitting, "I'm so glad you come; it seems so good to talk to somebody decent." She followed that with what must surely have been a confession in search of absolution: "I've been tough an' lived a bad life, an' like all them that makes mistakes I see it when it's too late. I'd like to be respectable, but nobody'll notice me; they say, 'There's old Calamity Jane,' an' I've got enough woman left 'bout me so that it cuts to hear them say it." Once more, Calamity broke down, crying. Fox said later she was sure the tears "were bitter with regret."

In concluding her article, Fox wondered outright "how much better anyone else would have done, placed in the same position." Calamity, she wrote, "has a kind heart, or her jolly good-natured manner belies her, and she has done a lot of good in the world."

Oddly enough, despite Calamity's self-bent efforts to efface her feminine nature, what she really seemed to thirst for more than anything else was the opportunity to live the, as she called it, "respectable life" of a pioneer woman. Had others taken the time to talk to Martha Jane Cannary, rather than being so quick to jump on the bandwagon of Calamity Jane's exploits, she might have evolved differently—more real, more honest, more sedate and settled with herself in her resignation to her dual personalities, often with conflicting responsibilities. She may well have turned out to be an entirely different woman.

Instead, as the dime novels and the tall tales kept plunging into her breast like a sharply honed piece of steel, she was forced to harden herself against the attacks and live up to the expectations. She had to become the Calamity she was, even if apparently not deep down inside.

If she hadn't, how different the world in which Calamity Jane rode would have been.

Chapter Twelve

A Star is Born

In 1893, Calamity Jane started to appear in Buffalo Bill's Wild West show as a storyteller. . . . Jane's addiction to liquor was evident even in her younger years . . . [when] she rented a horse and buggy in Cheyenne for a roughly one mile joy ride to Fort Russell and back, but Calamity was so drunk that she passed right by her destination without noticing it and finally ended up about 90 miles (140 km) away at Fort Laramie.

—*The Diaries of John Hunton: Made to Last, Written to Last*

In late 1895, after accepting an invitation to appear in Kohl and Middleton's Wild West show, Calamity decided to pose for some publicity shots. Stopping by the Locke and Peterson Studio in Deadwood, she was photographed in several different poses, seated and standing. The most popular of the selection showed a sturdy, stout woman dressed in a long, fringed buckskin coat and pants, a vest, and hat. She was looking straight into the camera. The photo proved to be a great seller throughout Calam's travels in the Black Hills, not to mention publicity for her shows.

A year later, Calamity posed for several additional photos in Livingston, Montana. Dressed in western garb as before, each of these shots portrayed the intrepid frontierswoman and showed Calamity holding a rifle. They became the quintessential representations of Calamity Jane, the Wild West Heroine who had scouted for General Crook and ridden as the companion of Wild Bill Hickok and Buffalo Bill Cody. Most importantly, though, they whetted the appetite of easterners who saw the photos republished in their own local newspapers in advance of an arriving show—with Calamity Jane herself, in the flesh!

But, while the publicity stills did wonders for advancing the name and legend of Calamity Jane, she soon decided she would need an even larger venue to draw in still bigger crowds. What better way to do so than to write (or have written) her very own autobiography!

Thus was born the *Life and Adventures of Calamity Jane, By Herself*. For the remaining seven and half years of her life, both as a performer and a roaming celebrity, she peddled her pamphlets and photographs wherever she traveled.

Of course, upon close examination, there's not a whole lot of truth in the pamphlet. In fact, the autobiography was a relatively unreliable source for Calamity's life; but it was far from without merit. The pamphlet not only offered helpful biographical hints as to Martha's early life but also provided the numerous sketches of her life on the prairie as she would have wanted it to be. (And, perhaps, *made* it be, if sometimes only in her own mind.)

The truth of the pamphlet is contained within the first couple of pages in which Jane provides confirmation of historical documentation regarding her birth in Missouri, the trip with her parents to Montana, and the wanderings of a young girl orphaned far too early in life, following the death of her parents. But her stretching of the truth begins on the very page in which she makes the false claim of having been with General George C. Custer at Fort Russell, Wyoming, in 1870. She also says she accompanied him to the southwest to fight Indians, returning to take part in the "Nursey Pursey Indian outbreak in 1872."

So far as a reality check goes, Calamity was never with Custer, who was not at Fort Russell or anywhere else in the southwest; and the Nez Perce conflict of 1872 didn't occur until 1877. In making all these "windy" claims, the autobiography, as historian James McLaird aptly notes, had "degenerated into frontier fiction."

But Calamity didn't stop her exaggerations there. Even though she never built up her personal relationship (aka her "love affair") with the western lawman "Hickock" [sic], Calamity claimed she was so upset by his murder that she "had grabbed a meat cleaver and made [Hickok's assassin, Jack McCall] throw up his hands." In reality, McCall's involvement in Hickok's murder is well documented.

Born in the early 1850s in Jefferson County, Kentucky, McCall eventually drifted west to earn his living as a buffalo hunter, a dirty, menial, grueling, and thankless job. By the time he landed in Deadwood, he had changed his name (for reasons unknown) to Bill Sutherland.

On August 1, 1876, McCall, after drinking at the bar at Nuttal & Mann's Saloon, sat in for a poker player who had dropped out of a game that included Wild Bill Hickok. Predictably, McCall, who was quite inebriated, proceeded to lose several hands in succession and wound up broke. Hickok offered the young man enough funds to buy breakfast and warned him not to play high-stakes poker again until he could afford the money he might lose. Although McCall accepted Hickok's charity, bystanders later said that Jack felt "insulted."

The following night, when McCall once again dropped into the saloon, another poker game was underway. Hickok faced away from the front door, in contrast to his regular practice of sitting in a corner with his back to the wall for his own protection. When McCall walked in and saw the lawman right in front of him, he pulled out a single-action .45-caliber revolver. Shouting, "*Damn you!*" he fired a single round into the back of Hickok's head. Hickok was dead before his body hit the floor.

McCall ran out of the saloon, attempting his escape on a stolen horse, but he fell from the animal, leaped up, and ran down the street on foot. He was soon discovered cowering in the rear of a local butcher shop and arrested.

The locals, incensed at the senseless assault on a local institution, called together an impromptu court composed of local miners, ranchers, and businessmen. McCall went on trial for his life the next day in a makeshift courtroom thrown together in McDaniel's Theater. The killer's defense was that his actions were justified: Hickok had gunned down his brother back in Abilene, Kansas. After a two-hour trial, the jury found McCall not guilty. The verdict prompted the *Black Hills Pioneer* to editorialize: "Should it ever be our misfortune to kill a man . . . we would simply ask that our trial may take place in some of the mining camps of these hills."

Following the dismissal, McCall, fearing for his safety, left Deadwood and headed into Wyoming Territory, where he continued his drinking binges while bragging about having killed the great "Wild Bill" in a fair gunfight. Wyoming authorities rearrested McCall after failing to recognize his acquittal for the killing based upon the grounds that Deadwood had no legal jurisdiction over the matter and, thus, McCall's acquittal was illegal. Officials agreed that, considering the circumstances, McCall could be tried again. The federal court in Yankton, Dakota Territory, agreed, advising that the "double jeopardy" standard did not apply. It set a date for a retrial.

McCall was tried once more for the murder, and this time he was found guilty. Some three months later, his time in jail ran out. He was hanged on March 1, 1877, at the ripe old age of twenty-four.

McCall was interred in Yankton's Sacred Heart Cemetery, which was moved in 1881. When his body was exhumed, witnesses claimed it still had the noose tied around its neck. McCall had the distinction of being the first person hanged by federal officials in the Dakota Territory.

That incident wasn't the only exaggeration to which Calamity Jane succumbed. Historians also doubt her rescue of a mail stage, delivering it safely into Deadwood after its driver, John Slaughter, had been killed by Indians, an oft-repeated claim made by Martha Jane.

Beside the historical inaccuracies in Calamity's autobiography, some personal references are also exaggerated or—dare it be said—even untrue. No independent confirmation exists that places the woman in California, southwestern United States, or Texas between 1883 and 1889; and Bill Steers, not Burke, was most likely the father of Jessie, who was born on October 29, 1887. If the "girl baby" was "the very image of its father," the father would have been Steers.

Calamity's autobiography does explain her plans to join a Western show and begin touring, but it fails to report that she had been planning on doing so since spring 1895.

Yet, regardless of whether or not the inaccuracies of the pamphlet were intentional, simple accidental misremembrances, or minor exaggerations in the author's mind, the booklet served its purpose of selling the image of Calamity Jane as a notorious Wild West woman. After all, who wouldn't want to see in person the woman who scouted for Generals Custer and Crook; helped capture murderer Jack McCall; and worked as a fearless and unparalleled stagecoach driver and bullwhacker? Whether or not the touring groups with whom she traveled during the latter years of her life played a part in the construction and support of the autobiographical musings is anybody's guess. Regardless, it's likely that the shows' promoters would have gladly touted the published material as true; for the bigger and brighter a star Calamity became, the more value she held for the shows.

So, following three months back in the Hills, Calamity set off on her tour with Kohl and Middleton. She had been contacted by a representative of the traveling group in Deadwood, and he invited her to become part of their "dime museums," which were popular history shows scattered throughout the country. A local newspaper reported that Calamity had signed an eight-week contract for fifty dollars a week, simply for agreeing to appear in several cities throughout the Midwest and East. Another report claimed that she had signed a one-year contract and would be visiting such sprawling metropolitan areas as Minneapolis, St. Louis, and even Chicago, on her way to the East Coast.

It was no little deal. Show owners Kohl and Middleton had designed their traveling venues from the ground up, utilizing the talents of veteran tour-show director George Middleton and his partner, C. E. Kohl. Before that, they had built a string of successful "dime museums" in the late 1800s. Relying upon a cadre of traveling "freaks" (horribly disfigured or physically unique people and animals), after the successes of original barnstormer P. T. Barnum, Middleton and Kohl launched their museums in cities ranging from Chicago, Milwaukee, and Cincinnati to Louisville, Minneapolis/St. Paul, and Cleveland. Most of them "paid handsomely," as Middleton later wrote in his memoirs. The museums, like Barnum's precursor circuses, professed to be "places of amusement" and education.

Most of the museums were built around two entities. The first was a permanent exhibit of mummies, petrified objects, and other unusually interesting artifacts. The second included the human element, consisting of musical performances, theatrical presentations, and human/animal "curiosities." In addition to the frontier plainswoman Calamity Jane, other human elements included the world-famous midget, Tom Thumb; illusionist/contortionist Harry Houdini; and "Big Winnie," a woman so overweight, she had to travel with the circus by railroad car. Compared to Big Winnie's earnings of three hundred dollars a week, Calamity's pay of fifty dollars seemed paltry.

A super-competitive arena, the dime museums had recently gotten a marketing shot in the arm when, three years earlier at the Columbian Exposition in Chicago, Buffalo Bill Cody's Wild West Arena pulled in hundreds of thousands of spectators. As many as twenty-five thousand visitors a day jammed the turnstiles to the extravaganza. That meant that, in its eight-month run, nearly five million people—or one in five visitors to the World's Fair—saw the show.

No doubt, Calamity's growing allure as an Old West star sprang from the shoulders of Cody's Wild West Show, as well as other competing groups. By the mid-1890s, Buffalo Bill had been on the road for a dozen years, taking his show to Europe and becoming one of the most recognized personalities in the world.

So in mid-January 1896 Calamity hopped a train for Minneapolis and her first performance for Kohl and Middleton. Clinton Burke, who had also been hired to work with the performers, was with her, while Jessie remained back home with the Ash family in Sturgis, attending school. As Calamity prepared to leave, she told the *Black Hills Daily Times* she didn't think she would "ever come to Deadwood again to remain any length of time." In Calam's mind, at least, a star was born.

Meanwhile, Kohl and Middleton, no strangers to sensationalism, quickly took to promoting their recent acquisition from the Wicked Wild West. In a poster commissioned for Calamity's inaugural debut at the Palace Museum in Minneapolis, they promised the world an extravaganza like none other—and threatened to deliver. They invited the public to come see up-close and personal "The Famous Woman Scout of the Wild West!—the Heroine of a Thousand Thrilling Adventures!—the Terror of Evildoers in the Black Hills!—the Comrade of Buffalo Bill and Wild Bill!" Exhorting the public that they simply had to see this "Famous

Woman and Hear Her Graphic Descriptions of Her Daring Exploits!,"
they exaggerated the billings just enough to whet people's appetites but
not enough to make them skeptical. And as if that wouldn't do the trick,
they hired the best graphic artists in the country to create the illustrations
to accompany the hyperbole.

Calamity's first show, on January 20, depicted her as a dangerous
woman, clad in buckskins with a rifle standing at the ready on her right
side and a vicious-looking knife clenched between her teeth.

After nearly a week of successful performances in Minneapolis, the
show pulled up stakes and set off for Chicago, where the sensationalism
continued. The same flyer with the same artwork appeared with Calamity
billed as "The Most Famous of All American Women," "Scout, Trapper
and Indian Slayer," and "The Woman who made Buffalo Bill eat his
words" with the "bravery of a lion and the tender heart of a woman."
Calamity was to appear at the Clark Street Dime Museum with, among
others, Ralston, the Rattlesnake King; Unzie, the Aboriginal Albino
Beauty; and Wm. Lee Roy, the "Nail King."

Records don't say how long Calamity's Chicago run was, but the
dramatic newspaper headlines continued to run each day for more than a
week. The *Chicago Daily Inter-Ocean* interviewed her and included several
fabrications in their article that they had picked up from her autobiography, as well as from her daily spiced-up presentations. The journalistic
portraits presented a remarkable woman from America's Wild West. As a
January 20 article in the *Inter-Ocean* wrote, "The most interesting woman
in Chicago at the present time arrived here Sunday night from the West."
The story said that Calamity had married a rancher ten years earlier, but
that he was by that time deceased (a logical, if inaccurate, inference, since
Burke by then had most likely left Kohl and Middleton). Calamity, the
paper said, was traveling and performing to keep her daughter in school
back in Deadwood. The adjacent ads touting Calamity's appearances
pitched her as a "Terror of Desperadoes, an Unerring Shot, and the Par-
ticipant in Many Lynching Bees."

The balance of Calamity's tour remains a mystery. She was in Chicago as late as February 9, expected to stay an additional week, but after
that, no more mention of her appeared in the newspapers. One reference

from Cincinnati suggests she may have been there in late February, in which case she most likely was still on tour. But she certainly terminated her contract at the end of May when she received a letter from Sturgis saying that Jessie was ill and needed her mother.

Regardless of what some historians report, Calamity was apparently quite successful on tour. Far from freezing up under the harsh lights of the stage, she seemed as comfortable spinning her yarns before sprawling audiences as she was leaning against a bar in Deadwood. Without training as an orator, she managed to overcome any semblance of stage fright. One Chicago newspaper reported that her shows were "proving very popular functions." Among her growing legions of fans were a significant number of women, which suggested, according to the reporter, "that heroine worship is quite as popular a fad as hero worship." Calamity certainly enjoyed the experience: "She tells in her simple manner the stories of her thrilling adventures among the redskins and of her experiences as a government scout." One member of her audience who knew Calamity from out west watched her performance and said, "She was the same old Calamity and kept her audience entertained all the time by her wit."

Nonetheless, her structured performances did vary in one respect from the tall tales she'd told back home. The Middleton and Kohl group promoted their show as family fare, so Calamity was forced to be on her best behavior. All "blue stuff was banned."

By early June, the *Black Hills Daily Times* reported that Calamity had returned from the East and planned to stay in the Hills for several months or more. Then she was to begin touring again in the fall. She had "proved to be a drawing card," which attracted the organizers of Huber's Palace Museum in New York City. For a woman named Calamity, her star was on the rise. The world lay at her doorstep. All she had to do was to open up the gate and let the world come waltzing in.

But could she?

Back in the Black Hills in 1896/97, Calamity resumed her rambling ways. For the next few years, she wandered around the northern West, mostly Montana. She tried earning a living by selling her photographs and pamphlet, although they brought in far less than she had hoped. The discouragement for a woman used to living alone and yet wanting to settle down to family life took a toll on the woman. As one year after another passed her by, her energy waned, as did her overall health. She seemed to do best when she was on someone's payroll, as she was in 1896 and would be again in 1901. She did poorest when left to her own devices. Perhaps that, too, is a reflection on her youth, on being abandoned to flounder around the West at such a young age while trying to provide some kind of future and care for her brother and sister. It was difficult enough for a young girl to survive in a male-dominated society when she came from a stable family and returned to a loving home each evening. It was virtually impossible for a waif such as Martha to grow and prosper without falling into a series of bad decisions and even worse situations. Just how reasonable can a twelve-year-old be expected to be?

So, predictably, Calamity Jane, just back from touring with Kohl and Middleton, resumed her nomadic lifestyle once more. After picking up Jessie in Sturgis, she continued traveling from pillar to post, spending time at first in Wyoming before moving on to Montana. Once there, she tried settling in and succeeded to a significant degree, although she rarely found work outside of her self-promotional efforts for more than a few days at a time.

On one of her first treks back after leaving the show, Calamity headed to Newcastle, Wyoming, where she claimed she intended to establish a home. But in a few days, she was spied in Sheridan, where she had a ruckus with a newspaper editor, warning him to keep her name out of his columns and to stop running stories on her every activity, as he'd done upon learning she'd come to town. Calamity didn't mind the press running tall tales about her life when *she* wanted them to, but when she didn't, the press was put on notice to "watch out"!

After that, Calamity called upon dentist Will Frackelton, who had heard of the legendary plainswoman but never before met her. He must have been frightened to death when he asked her to open her mouth so he could see what her problem was, not knowing what to expect on the heels of her far-flung reputation and recent run-in with the Sheridan newspaper editor. Frackelton later wrote of the incident at the newspaper that her words to the editor were "very much to the point." She didn't want any more publicity and so she "warned him profanely."

Naturally, upon seating the woman in his chair, Dr. Frackelton had "braced for a flood of billingsgate," but to his surprise, it failed to materialize. Instead, Calamity showed Side Two of a dual personality, carrying on a civilized conversation and insisting on paying the bill in silver. One of the dentist's friends, reflecting on her earlier attack on the city's editor and then her subdued demeanor in Frackelton's office, noted, "That's Calamity. When she wants to be a lady, she's as good as any of them. But let her get into a saloon or gambling joint and she'll outswear any man in the place."

The dentist later wrote of Calamity's appearance. She was, he said, "fairly good-looking, of average size, with red-hair streaked with gray." Her face was pock-marked and her "keen eye . . . seemed to go right through one." On her second visit to have several additional cavities filled, she was even more sociable, probably because she no longer felt threatened.

Frackelton wrote, "She was not an educated woman and profanity was as useful [to her] as the other words in her vocabulary. It simply dropped out naturally and never in an effort to seem hardboiled."

Frackelton concluded his observations about his most infamous patient by noting that the residents of Sheridan didn't quite know how to take her. Their "confused attitude" toward her was, on the one hand, due to her reputation as a hard worker and an angel of mercy throughout the towns and camps sprawled up and down the Rocky Mountains. On the other hand, she was equally renowned for her promiscuous behavior and profanity-laced epithets.

For Calamity's part, she was perfectly happy to be pain-free once more and eager to depart Wyoming for Montana. During some of her earliest sightings there, she had Clinton Burke and Jessie with her. Everything considered, one Montana reporter who had met Calamity years earlier wrote of her domesticity and how she had developed an increased "stoutness," evidence, he concluded, that the Wild Woman of the West was growing more mellow with the passage of time.

Another reporter with the *Anaconda Standard* preferred to focus his August 1896 story about Calamity's historical backdrop on her frontier days, concluding that "Calamity probably has a larger experience and more varied and checkered career on the frontier than any other woman of her class."

If such comments had gone only that far, Calamity would have been better served. Unfortunately, she was still her own worst enemy in that the seeds of sensationalism that she had sewn throughout the years continued to rise up to bite her. One story originating in the *Baltimore American* and reprinted from one coast to another revealed how little journalists knew or even cared about the truth of their subject's past, content instead to rely on her self-serving autobiography and larger-than-life promotions rather than digging into her past and fleshing out the woman's real personality. Most stories appearing about her began with headlines screaming about the "Devil Woman" who had killed more than five-score Indians and met and conquered a dozen bad men and who had even participated "in more deadly rows than falls to the lot of a hundred average men." Was the hyperbole true? Why should they care, believing (and rightly so), that Calam had put forth those statements herself—and for more years than anyone could recall.

And, of course, all the other "usual suspects" appeared within the pages of the Yellow Press—from Calamity's rescuing a stagecoach beset by Indians and capturing Jack McCaul (as one paper spelled his name) to helping string him up for the murder of Wild Bill Hickok. A particular favorite boasted of Calamity's daring rides with General Custer in the Nez Perce campaign of 1872/73 (even though the war didn't occur until 1877 and neither Calamity nor Custer played any role in it). The fact that the day's newspapers could, and *would*, publish such stories about an incident that occurred in Montana only two decades earlier is remarkable. Fake news, it appeared, had been around far longer than any respectable journalist would care to have admitted.

Not surprisingly, Calamity's reactions to such tall tales varied from mildly amused to viciously antagonistic, depending upon what purpose the stories served and whether or not that purpose was in keeping with the western figure's current goals. When she needed notoriety to help her blend into the rugged male-dominated countryside or, later, to draw crowds to see her presentations in a Wild West Show, she was happy with all the news she could muster. But when those days no longer suited her purpose, as when her daughter and husband looked to her to provide the glue to hold their domestic family unit together, she found them counterproductive and repugnant.

From August to November of 1896, Calamity, Burke, and Jessie visited the Montana towns of Livingston, Helena, Anaconda, Deer Lodge, and Castle. The number of short trips was possibly due to the new railroad spur, or short-branch, lines that helped to draw more riders to the main lines over time. Although not profitable in and of themselves, these new spurs helped to open up rural areas in already rural territories and states, including South Dakota, Wyoming, and Montana, making travel possible more quickly and efficiently than ever before. In her later years, when Calamity could no longer afford a ticket, she played cards with railroad agents to try to win her fare or simply implored them for a free ticket.

During her quick trips around the West, Calamity often talked about settling down. "I'm getting tired of always bein' on the move," a friend said she had confided in her. "I need a permanent place to settle." The local newspaper in Castle went so far as to claim that a couple by the name of "Mr. and Mrs. M. Burke" had actually opened a café there. But, without adequate capital, it quickly collapsed under its own financial weight. The Burkes were also credited with opening a boardinghouse or hotel, but it, too, soon folded. Adding to their frustrations due mostly to their inexperience as business owners, the couple reportedly got into legal trouble in Castle for failing to pay their bills.

Other news reports in spring and summer of 1897 concentrated more on Calamity's history, reminding readers that she had been one of the first women to travel to the Black Hills to witness firsthand the dramatic events unfolding there. One reporter, taking a shot at Calamity's autobiography, did so for its *lack* of stirring bravado as opposed to having too much. "Black Hillers . . ." he wrote, "regarded [the autobiography]

. . . as a very tame presentation of remarkably stirring facts." More than a month later, the Lewistown, Montana, newspaper reported that Calamity had come to town "for a couple of months" and was hawking the *Life and Adventures of Calamity Jane.* More newsworthy still, he added, she was preparing to rejoin the Kohl and Middleton show in early August. She was slated to appear in buckskins to "impersonate the female scout" of her remembrances, receiving a hundred dollars a month for her performances.

That same summer, after a brief stopover in Livingston, Calamity returned to Billings before departing to the Yellowstone Park area. It was an entirely new venue for the adventuress, and she was intent upon plumbing its riches for all she was worth. The railroad had opened up lucrative new environs that promised to yield exciting new sales for her photographs and pamphlets. She even went so far as to obtain a "Special Permit" to sell her memorabilia in the park.

From Yellowstone, Calamity traveled to the Gardiner area just north of the park, where she was rumored to have set up a "joy house" for lonely travelers, although no proof exists to that end. What is true is that at some point during her western travels, Calamity switched partners. Just as quietly as Clinton Burke had come into her life, he disappeared, and a new man, Robert Dorsett, entered her life. Burke wasn't heard from again in conjunction with Calamity after 1896/97, although his name did pop up in the Deadwood paper after the couple split up. Details are thin, although he was reported to be driving a hack—the equivalent of a modern-day taxi cab—there in the late 1890s. Despite developing a good reputation, he apparently fell upon tough financial times and was eventually accused by his employer of stealing some of the fare money he had taken in. By the time the employer found out, it was too late. As one Deadwood pioneer, John S. McClintock, put it, Burke "became an embezzler by appearing to trust his customers and making excuses for not turning in cash receipts, until his collections amounted to one hundred and seventy dollars. With this in his pockets he absconded and was never again heard of by either his family or his employer." Several years after McClintock confirmed the charge, Burke showed up again, this time in Texas, where he married and took a job as a watchman. He died in 1939 in Houston of throat cancer at sixty-two years of age.

By fall 1897 quietness had fallen over Calamity Jane just as the snows blanketed the park in its pristine purity. Jane, for some reason, remained incognito to the Montana, Wyoming, and South Dakota papers that so regularly ran updates on her life. But by the following summer, 1898, she exploded from her cocoon when she popped up in the most unlikely of places. In a June issue of the *Klondike Nugget*, a story ran about Calamity being in the northwestern Canadian province of the Yukon. How she got there or why she chose that locale is a mystery. The *Nugget's* articles were filled with a not unanticipated clash of revealing facts and questionable fancy. The first line of a story that appeared on June 23 contained a compilation of carefully distorted "truths." It began: Calamity Jane "of Deadwood and Leadville fame, and one of Wells Fargo's trusted detectives, is in Dawson." Of course, Calamity had spent little time in Leadville, and she'd never been a Wells Fargo detective. But that didn't deter the reporter, who continued by writing that Calamity's life had been one of "wild adventures," and "on more than one occasion she ha[d] been forced to take human life in defence of her own." Still, she "is as gentle and refined as any of her eastern sisters," although her "steel-blue eyes . . . warn the unwary, and a glance at the half-sad face indicates that her life has not been all sunshine."

Other newspaper accounts claimed that she had performed a bit while in the North Country, a statement that is untrue. None of the papers revealed that her time in the Yukon would be short, no more than a few days.

Two months later, Calamity reappeared in Livingston, once again peddling her photos and pamphlets, before moving farther east, showing up in Custer in southeastern Montana. As Calamity advanced through life into her early forties, she spent a good amount of time in 1898/99 in the Billings area, where she took numerous jobs, including house cleaning, fishing, gambling, and taking in the wash. When the railroad lines reached Billings in 1898/99, Calamity found both the ability and the excuse to travel around even more quickly than before. From Billings, she returned to the Yellowstone area, where she crossed paths with well-known travel writer Burton Holmes. A photograph he had taken shows an attractively attired Calamity selling her memorabilia there. Holmes described her as "the original, Simon-pure 'Calamity Jane,' who twenty years ago was famous as a woman-scout, and served our generals faithfully in many of the Indian wars."

Sometime during her time in Yellowstone, Calamity took Robert Dorsett for her next "husband." Not much about their relationship is documented except that, like Bill Steers and Clinton Burke before him, Dorsett was considerably younger than Calam—nearly twenty years so.

Perhaps their relationship generated so little press because it was purportedly short and stormy. In April 1899 the *Billings Gazette* declared that Calamity rolled into town from her most recent home in Bridger to check out some gossip that Dorsett had run off "with a young and handsomer girl." Dorsett at the time was working as a ranch hand and a laborer, freighting large containers of water to Bridger, just below Billings. One local rancher, Philip Korell, wrote later that Calamity and Dorsett had worked for him near Utica, where he claimed they remained for the better part of a year.

According to Korell, Calamity claimed that Dorsett was her husband and even referred to him as "Robert Dear, providing she was on the Water Wagon." When she wasn't, no one could predict her next move. On one occasion, the bartender of the Judith Hotel, on a dare, slipped into Calamity's room, stole some of her undergarments, and tacked them up over the bar. Learning of the affront, Calamity stormed in, brandishing a pistol beneath the bartender's nose, and promised to send him to the Great Beyond if he didn't take them down and apologize. Only after a series of intense negotiations during which the bartender promised Calamity free drinks for a week did Martha finally see the humor in the situation.

The most reliable source of information on Calamity during these months was provided by famed trail-drive cowboy E. C. (Teddy Blue) Abbott. Calamity bumped into him near Miles City after a span of nearly fifteen years. When they met in Gilt Edge, Teddy recalled he had borrowed fifty cents from her years before and wanted to repay her. She told him at the time of the loan, "I don't give a damn if you *ever* pay me."

Fifteen years later, Calamity accepted the repayment with one stipulation: The two of them would drink it up at the local saloon, which they did. When Blue asked her how she was faring with all the temperance people in town, trying to get her to turn over a new leaf, she teared up, downed the last of her drink, and looked him squarely in the eye. "Blue," she said, "why don't the sons of bitches leave me alone and let me go to hell my own route?"

Although records are unclear, Calamity's brief fling with Dorsett may have come to a premature end just short of the turn of the century. That's when Dorsett claimed that Calamity was incapable of fulfilling her parental responsibilities to Jessie and, under cover of darkness, spirited the girl away to live with his widowed mother in Livingston. Nothing more was said of the matter until years later, in the 1930s, when Jessie confessed that she had indeed left her mother's side over some unexplained irreconcilable differences.

Once again, it seems as if—with the rare exception of William Steers—Calamity did relatively well when her life was being directed by someone else—a "husband" or an employer or anyone who had a better grip on reality than the heroine of the plains had. Her life seemed most bucolic of all when she and Jessie were together with Burke. But when she was left alone to forge for herself, she always fell back into the same old trap that her parents had set for her years earlier and culminating with their deaths. Had they lived but a few years longer, they may have had time and the opportunity to instill in their oldest daughter the skill sets and traits required to make it alone in the West.

Or, maybe not.

Following her sudden abandonment by Dorsett and her own daughter, Calamity once more took to the road, although it's not certain where she went. One report places her in the town of Horr, near Yellowstone, in 1900. Bartender Billy Jump, noting that she was nearly destitute and in "awful shape," formed a committee of townsfolk to provide her with food and lodging through the winter. Jump encouraged her to spend her days drinking in his saloon while spinning improbable but, nevertheless entertaining, yarns for his patrons.

Another account placed her in the town of Columbus, where, according to legend, she spent parts of two winters. A local, young Jim Annin, put her up in the family's "pest house," which was a log hut for people who had contracted infectious diseases. There Calamity survived on only the bare necessities, buying only those items that she absolutely needed from Annin's father at the Columbus Mercantile and paying for them with cash. When spring rolled around and Calamity announced her plans to hit the trail once more, young Jim, who had always been leery of her legendary prowess with a six-shooter, said, "We breathed easier when winter broke earlier than usual and she had visited Columbus for the last time." He paused, as if recollecting, before adding, "A young lady who claimed to be her daughter, came to get her."

Toward the end of the year, Calamity most likely traveled to Montana, stopping off at Butte and Helena, where she spent a day or two in the Helena hoosegow, hallucinating, moaning, and shouting out to her young soldier companions to continue their valiant fight against the Indians.

Time and the ravages of a life roughly lived, it seemed, were finally catching up with Martha Jane Cannary. And alcoholism was only the beginning of the problems she was about to endure.

CHAPTER THIRTEEN

Turning of the Tides

And just at that very moment when the vast stretches of ocean threaten to engulf everyone and everything within their grasp, the tides suddenly reverse themselves, and the waters slowly begin to recede until, in the end, nothing is left at all except the place where the water once lived.

—ANONYMOUS

IN 1901 CALAMITY RETURNED TO MILES CITY AFTER AN ABSENCE OF nearly five years. But, in usual form, she didn't stay long. A succession of trips from January 3 to mid-February took her from Miles City to Billings, White Sulphur Springs, and Livingston. Everywhere she went, the warning signs were clear: Calamity wasn't well. Finally, in mid-February, she took gravely ill and, with no money for doctors, was admitted to the county poorhouse in Bozeman for several days. After she had recovered, she was dismissed and headed off once more to sell her photos and autobiography.

Even though Calamity's stay in the poorhouse was brief, it wasn't brief enough to avoid attracting the attention of the local press. The *Rocky Mountain Daily News* reported that Calamity had come to "such a poor pass in her old age that she has been compelled to apply for admission to the poor house in Gallatin county." The *Anaconda Standard* wrote that Calamity had "no friends [in Bozeman] nor money" and she "was sent to the poorhouse." It was the "first time in the eventful career of 'Calamity Jane' that she was obliged to accept aid from the county."

The *Rocky Mountain Herald* went even further, reporting that the Old West heroine would probably "end her melodramatic career in an almshouse." The reporter told readers that Calamity had "outlived a dozen husbands," had "killed as many Injuns as the next man," and "it was doubtful if she ever had a skirt on in her life." But now, the article continued, "poor old Calamity Jane has at last turned her back on all of her old-time glory and gone over the hills to the poorhouse."

All these "poorhouse" articles had an unexpected effect. People who knew Calamity—and even those who had only known her by reputation— poured their hearts out, emptying their pocketbooks along the way. Her supporters raised enough funds to assure that good ol' Calam would never again have to face the humiliating spectacle of county aid.

Following her stay in Livingston, she next journeyed to Red Lodge, Montana, and Cody, Wyoming, before returning again to Livingston in late April. There, she met writer Lewis Freeman, and his story—first published in *Sunset Magazine* and, after Calamity's death, as a chapter in a book entitled *Down the Yellowstone*—added a more human side to the legendary woman.

In every man's life there is one event that transcends all others in the bigness with which it bulks in his memory . . . . The thunderbolt of a living, breathing "Calamity Jane" striking at my feet from a clear sky is my biggest thing. One does his little curtsey to a lot of queens, real and figurative, in the course of twenty years' wandering, but not the most regal of them has stirred my pulse like the "Queen of the Plains." Queens of Dance, Queens of Song, and Queens of real kingdoms, cannibalistic and otherwise, there have been, but only one "Queen of the Rockies." And this was not because "Calamity Jane" was either young, or beautiful or good. (There may have been a time when she was young, and possibly even good, but beautiful—never.) So far as my own heart-storm was concerned, it was because she had been the heroine of that saffron-hued thriller called "The Beautiful White Devil of the Yellowstone" . . . which I had devoured in the hay-mow in my adolescence. The fragrance of dried alfalfa brings the vision of

"Calamity Jane" before my eyes even to this day. She is the only flesh-and-blood heroine to come into my life.

My initial meeting with "Calamity" was characteristic. It was a bit after midnight. On my way home to the old Albemarle to bed I became aware of what I thought was a spurred and chapped cowboy in the act of embracing a lamp-post. A gruff voice hailed me as I came barging by. "Short Pants!" it called; "oh, Short Pants—can't you tell a lady where she lives?"

"Show me where the lady is and I'll try," I replied, edging cautiously in toward the circle of golden glow.

"She's me, Short Pants—Martha Cannary—Martha Burk, better known as 'Calamity Jane.'"

"Ah!" I breathed, and again "Ah!" Then: "Sure, I'll tell you where you live; only you'll have to tell me first." And thus was ushered in the greatest moment of my life.

"Calamity," it appeared, had arrived from Bozeman that afternoon, taken a room over a saloon, gone out for a convivial evening and forgotten where she lived. She was only sure that the bar-keeper of the saloon was named Patsy, and that there was an outside stairway up to the second story. It was a long and devious search, not so much because there was any great number of saloons with outside stairways and mixologists called Patsy, as because every man in every saloon to which we went to inquire greeted "Calamity" as a long-lost mother and insisted on shouting the house. Then, to the last man, they attached themselves to the search-party. When we did locate the proper place, it was only to find that "Calamity" had lost her room-key. After a not-too-well-ordered consultation, we passed her unprotesting anatomy in through a window by means of a fire-ladder and reckoned our mission finished. That was the proudest night on which I am able to look back.

When, agog with delicious excitement, I went to ask after Mrs. Burk's health the following morning, I found her smoking a cigar and cooking breakfast. She insisted on my sharing both, but I compromised on the ham and eggs. She had no recollection whatever of our meeting

*of the previous evening, yet greeted me as "Short Pants" as readily
as ever. This name, later contracted to "Pants," was suggested by my
omnipresent checkered knickers, the only nether garment I possessed
at the time.*

*The "once-and-never-again 'Calamity Jane'" was about fifty-five
years of age at this time, [the author overcharged her by a decade]
and looked it, or did not look it, according to where one looked. Her
deeply-lined, scowling, sun-tanned face and the mouth with its
missing teeth might have belonged to a hag of seventy. The rest of
her—well, seeing those leather-clad legs swing by on the other side
of a signboard that obscured the wrinkled phiz, one might well have
thought they belonged to a thirty-year-old cowpuncher just coming
into town for his night to howl. And younger even than her legs was
"Calamity's" heart. Apropos of which I recall confiding to Patsy, the
bar-keep, that she had the heart of a young god Pan. "Maybe so,"
grunted Patsy doubtfully (not having had a classical education he
couldn't be quite sure, of course); "in any case she's got the voice of an
old tin pan." Which was neither gallant nor quite fair to "Calamity."
Her voice was a bit cracked, but not so badly as Patsy had tried to
make out. Another thing: that black scowl between her brows belied
the dear old girl. There was really nothing saturnine about her. Hers
was the sunniest of souls, and the most generous. She was poor all her
life from giving away things, and I have heard that her last illness
was contracted in nursing some poor sot she found in a gutter.*

*Naturally, of course, after a decent interval, I blurted out to
"Calamity" that I had come to hear the story of her wonderful life.
Right gamely did the old girl come through. "Sure, Pants," she replied.
"Just run down and rush a can of suds, and I'll rattle off the whole
layout for you. I'll meet you down there in the sunshine by those empty
beer barrels."*

*It was May, the month of the brewing of the fragrant dark-
brown Bock. Returning with a gallon tin pail awash to the gunnels,
I found "Calamity" enthroned on an up-ended barrel, with her feet
comfortably braced against the side of one of its prostrate brothers.
Depositing the nectar on a third barrel at her side, I sank to my*

ease upon a soft patch of lush spring grass and budding dandelions. "Calamity" blew a mouth-hole in the foam, quaffed deeply of the Bock, wiped her lips with a sleeve, and began without further preliminary: "My maiden name was Martha Cannary. Was born in Princeton, Missouri, May first, 1848." Then, in a sort of parenthesis: "This must be about my birthday, Pants. Drink to the health of the Queen of May, kid." I stopped chewing dandelion, lifted the suds-crowned bucket toward her, muttered "Many happy Maytimes, Queen," and drank deep. Immediately she resumed with "My maiden name was Martha Cannary, etc." ...

Here, little dreaming what the consequence would be, I interrupted, and for this reason: I had felt that "Calamity" had been doing herself scant justice all along, but in the "christening" incident her matter-of-fact recital was so much at variance with the facts as set down in "The Beautiful White Devil of the Yellowstone" that I had to protest. "Excuse me, Mrs. Burk," I said, "but wasn't that officer's name Major Piercy Darkleigh instead of Egan? And didn't you cry "For life and love!" when you caught his reeling form? And didn't you shake your trusty repeater and shout "To hell with the redskins!" as you turned and headed for the fort? And didn't you ride with your reins in your teeth, the Major under your left arm and your six-shooter in your right hand? And when you had laid the Major safely down inside the Fort, didn't he breathe softly, "I thank thee Jane from the bottom of a grateful heart. No arm but thine shall ever encircle my waist, for while I honour my wife——"

Here "Calamity" cut in, swearing hard and pointedly, so hard and pointedly, in fact, that her remarks may not be quoted verbatim here. The gist of them was that "The Beautiful White Devil of the Yellowstone" was highly coloured, was a pack of blankety-blank lies, in fact, and of no value whatever as history. I realize now that she was right, of course, but that didn't soften the blow at the time.

Here, forgetting myself, I interrupted again in an attempt to reconcile the facts of "Wild Bill's" death as just detailed with the version of that tragic event as depicted in "Jane of the Plain." "Calamity's" language was again unfit to print. "Wild Bill" had not expired with his head on her shoulder, muttering brokenly "My heart was yours from the first, oh my love!" Nor had she snipped off a lock of Bill's yellow hair and sworn to bathe it in the heart-blood of his slayer. All blankety-blank lies, just like the "White Devil...."

"Calamity" had been delivering to me her museum tour lecture, that which had also been printed in a little pink-covered leaflet to sell at the door. That was why, like a big locomotive on a slippery track, she had had to back up to get going again every time she was stopped. Oh, well, the golden dust from the butterfly wing of Romance has to be brushed off sometime; only it was rather hard luck to have it get such a devastating side-swipe all at once. That afternoon for the first time I began to discern that there was a more or less opaque webbing underlying the rainbow-bright iridescence of sparkling dust.

With "Calamity Jane," the heroine, evanishing [sic] like the blown foam of her loved Bock, there still remained Martha Burk, the human document, the living page of thirty years of the most vivid epoch of Northwestern history. Compared to what I had hoped from my historic researches in the pages of "The Beautiful White Devil of the Yellowstone," this was of comparatively academic though none the less real interest. Reclining among the dandelions the while "Calamity" oiled the hinges of her memory with beer, I conned through and between the lines of that record for perhaps a week. Patiently diverting her from her lecture platform delivery, I gradually drew from the strange old character much of intimate and colourful interest. Circulating for three decades through the upper Missouri and Yellowstone valleys and gravitating like steel to the magnet wherever action was liveliest and trouble the thickest, she had known at close range all of the most famous frontier characters of her day. Naturally, therefore, her unrestrained talk was of Indians and Indian fighters, road-agents, desperadoes, gamblers and bad men generally—from "Wild Bill" Hickock and "Buffalo Bill" Cody to Miles and Terry and Custer, to "Crazy Horse," "Rain-in-the-Face," Gall and "Sitting Bull." She told me a good deal of all of them, not a little, indeed, which seemed to throw doubt on a number of popularly accepted versions of various more or less historical events. I made notes of all of her stories on the spot, and at some future time of comparative leisure, when there is a chance to crosscheck sufficiently with fully established facts from other sources, I should like to make some record of them. These pages are not, of course, the place for controversial matter of that kind.

One morning I kept tryst among the dandelions in vain. Inquiry at the saloon revealed the fact that "Calamity," dressed in her buckskins, had called for her stabled horse at daybreak and ridden off in the direction of Big Timber. She would not pay for her room until she turned up again, Patsy said. It was a perfectly good account, though; she never failed to settle up in the end. I never heard of her again until the papers, a year or two later, had word of her death.

After securing with him her story—much of which is obviously true and the rest just as apparently fancied, Calamity increased the frequency and volume of her drinking. By that May she was virtually out of control, and she took sick once more. Observers wondered if death was imminent. But Calamity managed to keep the beast at bay through her own resilience and determination. Once well again, she resumed her calling as a traveling saleswoman, once again visiting Yellowstone Park to peddle her photos and autobiography to unsuspecting but utterly thrilled tourists.

By then the earlier poorhouse stories had fanned the flames of indignation across the nation. Finally, they reached the eyes of an ambitious eastern woman named Josephine Winifred Brake. A tireless researcher and promoter, Brake—yet one more hand from the abyss reaching out to pluck the wayward canary from its doom—was about to turn Calamity's life around.

When Josephine Brake, an easterner, read the poorhouse stories about one of America's most revered legendary figures, she was moved. So much so that she decided to travel west, find Calamity (not at all an easy task in itself!), and talk her into coming back east with her, where her financial future would be secured. Of course, Brake may also have had a more pecuniary rationale for securing the services of Calamity Jane—and most likely did. Still, her perseverance goes beyond the usual money-making schemes to someone who was genuinely concerned about Calamity in her declining health and dwindling years left on earth.

Brake arrived in Butte in early July 1901 and, as predictability would have it, Calamity was nowhere to be found. Moving on to Livingston, the woman enlisted the help of Dell Alderson, editor of the *Livingston Post*, to search for Martha. A short while later, the *Post* reported that Brake had found Calamity "ill in the hut of a negro woman on the bank of the Yellowstone." According to Alderson's account, Brake's first words to Calamity were, "I'se been waitin', honey, waitin' long for you. Come along east with me and I'll set you up in business and put you on the cushions for the rest of your natural life."

At hearing the offer and seeing the sincerity in the woman's eyes, Calamity broke down and cried "bitter, burning, boiling tears all over the ill-kept cot on which she was lying." Overwhelmed with Brake's generosity, according to Alderson, Martha promised "to be a good girl all the rest of her life."

In a subsequent issue of the *Post*, a reporter explained Martha's most recent illness as the result of her hiking three miles over mountainous terrain every day to aid a friend who'd been confined in the Aldridge hospital with blood poisoning. As the story went, Martha had carted fruit and other necessary items to the invalid. She used proceeds from her photograph and booklet sales to finance the goods. During her last trip, Martha fell ill and "took to her bed, where she was found by her benefactress."

But not all newspapers bought into the unbridled generosity of Mrs. Brake. The *Billings Times* ran a headline reading, "Gone Off In Doubtful Company," saying that many old timers were concerned about Martha being "railroaded out of the state of Montana by an entire stranger." The reporter said he had gotten suspicious of Brake's intentions when she accidentally admitted to being a reporter for the *New York Journal.* Later, upon further questioning, she denied it. The *Times* reported:

Newspaper women do not receive such magnificent salaries that they can make such journeys and burden themselves with the care of an old woman. She never saw Jane; only read about her. She has some scheme afoot and Calamity will bitterly regret leaving Montana. She will earn what she gets, but only for the woman who took her away.

Some of the old pioneers ought to try and keep watch as to just where Calamity is taken.

Other reporters ran similar pieces. One for the *Red Lodge Picket* predicted that "the old girl won't take kindly to this eastern scheme. . . . Calamity, you know, likes pilgrims at about the same ratio that the devil is stuck on holy water." Similarly, the *Butte Miner* thought it "doubtful if 'Calamity Jane' will take to this radical change" and speculated that she'd be back haunting the towns of Montana before year's end.

An editor for the *Billings Gazette* opined about the ironic circumstances surrounding Calamity's dichotomous life. She was being handed the chance to retire in eastern luxury for the rest of her days because of who she was. But Calamity was "who she was" only because of the dime novels and writers of the "yellow backs," he said, even though she denounced them as nonsense and lies. Had she been forced to fend for herself based upon the *real* Martha Jane—aka Calamity—she would never have gotten the opportunity that Brake ultimately offered her.

Martha, he said, was not a scout or an Indian fighter as had been claimed but, rather, a camp follower who showed up at various posts around the West—right around payday, propitiously enough. He went on to say that the "picture of 'Calamity,' clad in buckskin reining wild charger and waving a man's hat as she led a band of dashing troopers into battle" was pure fiction. It had little to do with the real-life character of Martha Cannary.

Although the editor had serious misgivings about the tall tales involving Martha's "military career," he acknowledged her many redeeming qualities. "Her deeds of unselfish charity and benevolence . . . atoned for many of her shortcomings." And those shortcomings nearly always involved her abuse of alcohol. Nonetheless "when the time comes that she must answer for her deeds on earth the good recorded to her credit will be found to balance the bad."

But while the area writers reflected upon the circumstances behind Martha's announced departure, Calamity was busy making preparations for the journey. First and foremost, that meant joining the boys for a good-bye drink. Or two. After that, she loaded her belongings on the coach and left with her new chaperone. At a brief layover in Glendive, a reporter who had gotten wind of her passage stopped Martha to ask her a question about the wisdom of her decision. "She said she had no regret leaving the scenes that had made her famous, because no one in this part of the country cared for her now."

But the marriage made in heaven between Martha and Brake soon began to sour. By the time they had traveled to St. Paul and registered at the Ryan Hotel, Brake was described by a local reporter as "extremely nervous." He added that traveling with Martha must have been "equal to a tenderfoot's first experience with a bucking broncho." Although Martha had agreed to abstain from drinking "except when Mrs. Brake consented," Martha badgered her so often that Brake usually gave in. "The flask," according to the *St. Paul Dispatch*, "had been worn as smooth as a nursing bottle." The newspaper went on to admit that Calamity was "no stranger to corn juice and about four times a day," but as long as she let Brake know about her imbibing, there was no problem. She was also smoking big black cigars, the article alleged.

During their layover in St. Paul, Brake had bought Calamity some new clothes and face powder to make her appear more feminine. Martha, after going to her room to dress, emerged with powder scattered "in promiscuous fashion on her bright blue shirtwaist black skirt, face and hair," according to one journalist, insisting that she "was a sight to behold when Mrs. Brake opened the door and surveyed her." Detracting from Calamity's overall image of pulchritude were the "long, black cigars" she did indeed chain-smoke from one end of the country to the other. When questioned by the press about Calamity's obstinate refusal to polish her image, Brake said only that Martha was "honesty personified" and did not pretend to be anything other than herself. Still, it's a safe bet that Brake found Martha to be a handful.

And they weren't the only ones. After arriving in Minneapolis, Martha proudly held out a battered satchel for a writer's inspection. She told him it had gotten battered from banging it over the head of a Montana reporter whose works Martha deemed to be total fabrications. "He didn't see me," Martha said, "and I got a good crack at him. His head was cut considerable." That correspondent never did get to finish his interview.

Brake, far from being horrified at her protégé's actions, knew that, if she were to continue to snag publicity for Martha, she would have to do it in a way to which Martha wouldn't object. Instead of introducing her to the next erstwhile reporter to come along, Brake told Martha the man was her cousin and advised her to get to know him.

And the ruse seemed to work. Martha and Brake's "cousin" were having a grand old time conversing about Martha and her experiences out west when suddenly a fellow reporter from a rival newspaper entered the room and asked Martha for an interview.

"I give you to understand that I don't give no news to papers," she snapped. "You git right out of here." The reporter pointed to his compatriot and said, "I don't see why you won't talk to me. Our paper is just as good as the one this man represents."

Realizing that she had been duped, Martha exploded. Searching the "cousin" for the notes he tried to conceal, she ripped them to pieces and flung them across the room, ordering both reporters out while peppering the air with "a few choice expletives, large octagonal ones," according to a local reporter. The entire charade couldn't have helped endear Brake to Calamity.

Nevertheless, Calamity seemed willing to forgive and forget, and the unlikely twosome continued on their journey together to Buffalo, New York. Brake had secured a short-term rental home for Martha. The next evening Martha went through her routine for her very first eastern venue, and the crowd went wild; it went so well, in fact, that the *Buffalo Morning Express* reported on July 29 that a trip to Niagara Falls was next on Martha's itinerary. She was to be joined by poet Ella Wheeler Wilcox and General Egan. Martha also met "Doc" Waddell, press agent for Colonel Fred Cummins's Indian Congress, a competing Wild West show performing at the Pan-American Exposition in Buffalo. "Possibilities of new calamities undoubtedly rose in the imagination of Doc, as he gazed on Jane," remarked a local newspaperman.

The *Cummins Indian Congress and Wild West Show* was originally organized and put together by Col. Fred T. Cummins for the 1901 Pan American Exposition. He soon found it to be so popular with his audiences that he decided to keep the show running, making it a permanent part of his Wild West repertoire. The show was still alive and active in 1904 at the St. Louis World's Fair.

Cummins, who had assembled representatives from thirty-one Native American tribes in 1898 for the Trans-Mississippi Exposition, did so again for the 1899 Omaha Greater American Exposition. From these successful performances, he created his Pan-American Exposition show featuring "leading chieftains from forty-two different tribes of North American Indians." Among these, Geronimo received top billing.

Cummins hoped to add Martha to his show and chartered the trolley car that took him, Brake, and Calamity to Niagara Falls. During the visit, Martha "stood on the brink of the falls and her photograph was taken as she seemed to defy the waters," one newspaper reported. During that time, Cummins and Calamity hit it off, and not much after, the Indian Congress announced that Calamity Jane had been adopted "as one of the members of the [show]." Brake's involvement in swinging Calamity over to the Indian Congress is only speculation; but she apparently played a major role in the negotiations. Since Martha's wages included a hefty "managerial fee" paid to Brake, the more Calamity made, the more her benefactor raked in. Naturally, Martha agreed to several stipulations limiting the amount of her drinking, carousing, and even traveling without prior permission.

Still, things were looking good from Martha's perspective. On the night before her first performance in Cummins's show, she was the guest of honor at a reception banquet held at the swank Iroquois Hotel. Many of the East's most prominent people attended. They were anxious to see up close and personal this legendary show woman and true western heroine "who had passed through the stirring times of the Far West."

Nevertheless, the *Buffalo Enquirer* reported that at the party, Calamity seemed "rather out of atmosphere." She "wore her battlefield attire . . . the buckskin trousers and beaded blouse of chamois . . . capped by a sombrero." Another Buffalo newspaper observed that the speeches about Calamity at the reception indicated that "her word is as good as her bond and she was loved and respected by everybody in the West."

Colonel Cummins may have been ahead of his time—or at least he was on par with Buffalo Bill Cody and his Wild West Show. But his actions may have been a bit more tinged with financial concerns: Told of Calamity's traveling east to the Buffalo Exposition, he "hastened to secure her for his concession [the Indian Congress] and succeeded in closing a contract."

Regardless, at the party, Martha was anything but a gracious guest. One reporter said she "made a short speech at the reception," but "would say nothing at table, following an old western scout's custom of keeping silence at public functions." That evening, it was announced that Martha would drive a hundred-mule train down Buffalo's Main Street the following afternoon. "This will be the biggest mule team ever hitched up," a reporter wrote, and "Calamity Jane will handle it just as easily as an ordinary teamster handles a span of trained horses."

That turned out to be true. In fact, Calamity became an increasingly popular part of the Cummins Indian Congress. Cummins's troupe of performing artists included numerous Indian clans in all kinds of dress and situations. For Cummins, who had long stressed the diversity of Indian life and cultures in his shows, something was missing. Finally, it dawned on him that what his shows lacked was *drama*. Calamity was to provide a more dramatic component—that of a sensational western character straight out of the pages of history.

Meanwhile, behind the scenes—just as Martha's old Montana friends had predicted, Calamity's "life of ease" had eroded away, replaced by a grueling schedule to showcase her talents. Brake, while not exactly guiltless in leading Calamity astray, nonetheless began working to secure a government pension for Martha, who was "as much entitled to a pension as any man who fought for the Government." Just in case.

The Pan-American Exposition, composed of shows and exhibits from various states and countries throughout the Western Hemisphere, had opened to hundreds of thousands of visitors from around the world. That summer, President William McKinley, Vice President Theodore Roosevelt, Austria's Kaiser Wilhelm, Admiral George Dewey, and General Nelson A. Miles all attended. Special days were designated to honor organizations in attendance. July 31 was "Elks Day," when costumed members of the Benevolent and Protective Order of Elks (B.P.O.E.) marched through the city's streets. It was in this parade that Martha drove "a watering cart" drawn by a hundred mules.

She had been strategically situated near the end of the procession so that, by later that afternoon, the Elks were treated to a special performance by the Indian Congress. Martha "was given a warm reception, and her riding was good enough to ensure her success with every audience that sees the show," one reporter wrote. Another guest star was "Wenona, the Sioux girl sharpshooter," who shot holes in a placard spelling out B.P.O.E. "on a target with rifle bullets" for the attendees.

Several journalists expressed the feeling that Calamity's performance in Cummins's exhibition proved that Brake was exploiting her. In some weeks, Martha was alleged to receive less than a dollar plus her meal expenses.

Making her second parade appearance on "Midway Day," more than a hundred thousand visitors to the exposition turned out. The parade's Grand Marshal was Frederick T. Cummins, himself. The stars consisted of the Carlisle Indian Band and "Calamity Jane, the heroine, who wears a hero's garb," according to the local newspaper. After Martha's billing came Geronimo, described by one reporter as the "old fellow on the gray horse who was followed by three fierce Apaches in light yellow."

According to the local newspapers, Martha was a big star of the Cummins's show. "The arrival of Calamity Jane at the Indian Congress has stirred things to greater activity," one reporter wrote. "Every day during the past week the congress had an attendance comprising nearly one-half of the total number of people who past [sic] through the main entrances of the Pan-American."

Cummins's success was attributable to yet other reasons, including the fact that the Indian Congress was an open-air performance in a sprawling arena seating nearly twenty-five thousand people. The Congress also included typically western events such as "expert rifle shooting, Indian races of all kinds, Wild West sports and pastimes, and a mighty sham battle participated in by 500 warriors." In addition, the Indian Congress was promoted as "one of the Government's contributions" to the exposition. The "700 Indians which are a part of the congress are here by special permission from the United States Government."

Not surprisingly, with all the promotional hyperbole, the nation's love affair with the sprawling American West was *the* biggest attraction for visitors. As one local newspaper noted, the show tugged at America's heart and appealed "to the school boy who loves to delve into books of daring and adventure of frontier times in the old days." Of all the attractions, though, the reporter noted the most appreciated to be "Geronimo, the human tiger, Winona, the wonderful Sioux rifle shot, and Calamity Jane, famous in song and story of frontier days."

Calamity's drawing power was especially notable, since Cummins's flyers and advertisements never mentioned her by name, most likely since she had joined the show after all the handouts had been printed. Cummins did manage to feature her, though, in a 1902 flyer that included pictures and descriptions of the daring people who starred in his extravaganzas and devoted most of its space to Calam. Most of the attributes he painted of her turned out to be false—she had been a spy during the Civil War, passing as a male by wearing men's garments, for example. (Calamity was nine years old when the war broke out in 1865!) The brochure also incorrectly alleged that Calamity "was never connected with any other public exhibition." That statement, too, was false.

Still, in the end, all the manufactured bravado may only have served them both better. In the photographs taken of her at the exposition, Martha appeared to be an aging, sober-looking woman who was not particularly happy with her plight in life. That, of course, wouldn't have been much of a stretch.

One day, just before a performance, one of Martha's old friends from Montana, W. H. Newcom (Wirt), turned up to see his old pard perform. As Newcom and his friends and family entered the grounds, shooting suddenly broke out in the distance. Newcom recalled someone saying, "O, that is the Wild West show. Do you want to go in there with us? They have that wonderful woman with the show; I think they call her Calamity Jane. Did you ever hear of her in the West?" When Wirt explained that she was an old acquaintance from back home, his family went crazy, insisting on meeting her. He tried to explain that "'Jane' was a bit rough," but his relatives wouldn't hear of it.

Finally, when the performance had nearly come to an end—a "very good" show, as Wirt recalled—Martha came barreling into the ring on horseback, whooping and hollering as only she could, her buckskin clothes chattering in the breeze. She "stole the show," Wirt reported later; and, true to his words, he took his relatives to see her in her quarters afterward. When Martha finally spied him, she called out, "Slim. Old Slim from Miles City. Damn my skin, if it ain't. Where in h*** did you—?" Newcom quickly hushed her up, whispering that his relatives were there and that they were all staunch Christians.

Never will I forget poor old Jane, and never was I more amazed at any change of front in a person; never could you imagine it could by any chance be the same person I had just met in the rough, boisterous way. I stopped sweating blood. I was too delighted with her and she was as polite as any one of the party and entertained them all royally for fifteen or twenty minutes.

Before parting ways, Calamity vented to Wirt the difficulty she was having with Brake. She told him she doubted she could survive all of her restrictions, not the least of which involved her drinking. We can only speculate about what Wirt had advised her to do—and with what choice of words!

Whatever he told her, evidently his advice carried some weight. Martha and Brake had reached an impasse. According to one news report, Martha felt Brake and others were keeping the majority of her wages, paying her only pennies on the dollar. That might have been improper business practice, taking advantage of a woman "uneducated" in the world of high finance. But it might also have been good old common sense, keeping money out of Martha's hands that she would only have squandered on liquor, cigars, and parties.

Perhaps, though, the truth lay in the middle. A barely mentioned reference to Brake suggests that she was in the employ of the Pan-American Exposition and had worked out an agreement with them to deliver the one and only Calamity Jane into their hands, similar to the situation with Geronimo. If that were true, Brake would have benefitted, Calamity would have benefitted, and the exposition people would have benefitted most of all.

So, the die was cast. By removing Brake as her agent and negotiating directly with Cummins, Martha "got real money" while escaping the philanthropist's strict prohibitions against drinking and "catting around." From that point on, Martha was free as a bird, free of Brake. But for good or bad? Only time would tell.

Sure enough, without the restraints by which Brake had shackled her protégé, Martha was soon back to her old tricks. "Alas, 'Calamity Jane,' The Aged Celebrity, Overcome by Liquor, Arrested, and Released on Suspended Sentence," screamed one Buffalo newspaper's headline. "Mrs. Mattie Dorsett, the original 'Calamity Jane,' of Wild West fame," the article continued, was discovered by a patrolman near the exposition gate "reeling from side to side." Although Martha spent the night in jail, she received a suspended sentence the next morning. As the paper alleged in Jane's defense, "it was the first time she had ever been arrested."

—◦—

The press back home in Montana, of course, had a field day. They could have predicted (and, in fact, many of them did) what Jane would do the day she was in receipt of her very first full paycheck. The *Livingston Post* reprinted the colorful account from the *New York Sun*: After receiving her pay, Martha "passed out of the grounds. Across from the gates the door of a saloon stood invitingly open. Jane passed in." What came next was similarly predictable, if not particularly newsworthy back home: "What Jane does in saloons is a matter of history," the author of the piece concluded. "It need not be reported."

Although Martha had received a suspended sentence on her first arrest in Buffalo, she insisted on pushing her luck. The day after her incarceration, when an exposition guard "attempted to interfere with her personal liberty," he "was sent spinning on his head." During yet one more saloon brouhaha, Jane was said to turn "the atmosphere blue." She was hauled before the court and "admonished to sin no more." But sin she did, one of her sprees said to be the result of a broken relationship. Martha had apparently met and fallen in love with a man named Frederick Darlington from Batavia, New York. He had supposedly reciprocated her feelings, although it's not clear as to what degree. When Jane finally realized "the hopelessness of her passion" and the inaccessibility of her "man," she locked herself in her room for three days. When her self-confinement had expired, she "went on the warpath in regular frontier style and made things lively around the Indian village." The spree ended only after Darlington showed up to comfort her. One edition of the *Billings Times* went so far as to predict in its September 5, 1901, edition that the sound of wedding bells would soon fill the eastern air. If so, Calamity hadn't heard them.

Not long after, Calamity made up her mind to leave the East behind. She longed for the sparse open spaces of the western frontier. She belonged back in Montana, South Dakota, and Wyoming, where the people were real, and phoniness didn't exist. But she had no money. Recalling that an old friend by the name of Byron Hinckley had extended an invitation to her to visit him if she was ever in Pennsylvania, she caught a ride to English Centre, where her friend had relocated. During her four-day visit, a local stable caught fire and burned to the ground. A chestnut horse that Martha had grown fond of had to be put down because of severe burns.

Martha, thinking back over a previous experience she'd once had with a fortune-teller, apologized to Hinckley. When he asked why, she said the soothsayer had foretold: "No matter how evenly your life stream seems running, suddenly it dams up, there will always be death, fire and ruin wherever you are." Looking down as she fought back a well of tears, Martha added, "I couldn't even keep my child with me."

Hinckley never blamed Martha for the fire, of course; but her comments led him to believe that she somehow felt personally responsible. Martha Jane left Pennsylvania shortly after.

The newspapers back in Montana had learned of Martha's desire to return home but said she was short of funds. She hoped famed showman William F. Cody, scheduled to arrive soon in Buffalo with his show, might help her. Finally, when Buffalo Bill's Show hit town, a Great Parade was thrown to welcome them and drum up ticket sales. Cummins's Indian

Congress joined the procession, but none of the news reports of the parade mentioned Calamity Jane. Finally, one newsman reported that, shortly after Cody's arrival, "a very tired and despondent looking woman pushed aside the curtains" of his tent. Martha, who had met Cody years earlier on the trail, told him, "They've got me Buffaloed, and I wanter go back. There's no room for me in the east. Stake me to a railroad ticket and the price of the meals, an' send me home." Cody purchased a train ticket for her and threw in an extra twenty-five dollars for food. Later, according to a newspaper report, "Calamity Jane disappeared, and it is supposed she is using the ticket."

In comments he made nearly a year later, Cody recalled that Jane "was anxious to leave Buffalo," but lacked the money to do so. The police were equally anxious to see her go. Cody felt obligated to help, "for her sorrows seemed to need a good deal of drowning, and she got into lots of trouble." He helped her out, he said, because "she was one of the pioneers. For old time's sake, you know."

Martha's departure from Buffalo took place only days before President McKinley was scheduled to arrive for a celebration of President's Day. Cummins's Indian Congress had arranged for a special ceremonial performance in his honor. But on Friday, September 6, while McKinley spoke at the exposition fairgrounds, anarchist Leon Czolgosz pulled out a pistol and shot him at point-blank range. Eight days later, the president was dead. Czolgosz was reportedly motivated by Emma Goldman, an anarchist leader, whose lecture he had attended earlier in Cleveland. The event caused one Montana correspondent to lament, "Calamity may not be possessed of all the feminine graces, but she is a better citizen than Emma Goldman any day in the week."

By that time, Martha's travels had taken her as far away from Buffalo as Chicago, where she found herself alone and broke. Most likely she had been stranded, orphaned by her own foolish squandering of the funds Cody had provided for her return home. Having few other options, Calamity signed a contract to appear at a dime museum in the Windy City. When an acquaintance from Billings stumbled upon her there, she "embraced him as if she had found a long lost brother." Imploring him to help her out, Martha said the New York benefactor had secured her "for exhibition purposes" and not at all to provide her with a life of leisure. Neglecting to mention Cody's help, Martha contracted with the Chicago dime museum to "accumulate enough money to pay her railway fare back to Montana." But she found getting sufficient funds together difficult. So she went on performing until she had raised enough money to carry her as far west as Minneapolis, where a theatrical publication promoted her appearance at the Palace Museum, where she had performed in 1896: "Hear Calamity Jane tell of her wild life fighting Indians on the frontier."

As coincidence would have it, while standing at the corner of Nicollet Avenue and Second Street, Martha ran into the reporter who had lied to her about being Brake's cousin only a few weeks earlier. Martha was stunned when he asked her to grant him another interview.

"Not in a hundred years!" she shot back, calling him a lying cur and unleashing a string of slurs peppered with a "storm of invectives." A crowd gathered and a policeman had to intervene so Martha could continue on her way. The *Minneapolis Star* reported the journalist's reaction: "*Wh-e-w!* Guess that's about near enough to get to her. Thought sure she was going to strike *me.*" Martha, her pockets jingling with a new influx of cash, left Minnesota none too soon following her confrontation.

In the meantime, back west, the Montana papers made note of Martha's agonizingly slow progress toward her return home, finally predicting her arrival within a week or two. But Martha, never one to be outguessed, had disappeared. On a whim, she had decided to visit her earlier stopping-off place in Pierre, South Dakota.

"Calamity Jane is back for a visit at her old stamping grounds when Pierre was the jumping off place for civilization and west of it was hostile country," reported a local newspaper that November. "The old timers who she is looking up mostly agree that she is the genuine Jane who lived here twenty years ago," adding, nonetheless, that "there are those who are doubtful and claim that the original Jane is dead." Shockingly, several of Pierre's reporters were woefully ignorant of Jane's recent fiasco out east. When she popped up in Pierre, most of the young pups naturally assumed that she was on a short jaunt "from the Hills country." Martha announced that she intended to remain in Pierre for the coming winter.

At first, Martha's life in Pierre was pretty tame. But in time, that changed. "Evidently [she] does not want the public to get an idea that she is tottering over the precipitous verge of toothless decrepitude and aged decay merely because she is not so young as she used to be," one observant if excessively poetic Pierre journalist wrote. After drinking "a quantity of hopified elixer," she assaulted a man "with a yard or so of pyrotechnic billingsgate and vituperative epithets, which she uncoiled with the glibbest of tongues and which will make his hair crimp when he thinks of it ten years from now," the Pierre wordsmith concluded. "Since her tea parties are not of the kind to meet the unqualified approval of the best society of Pierre, since it became the capital of the state, it is hoped that she will confine her operations to a limited area."

"Still on Earth," screamed the Livingston newspaper headline after the editor learned of Martha's antics in Pierre. "Several weeks ago the newspapers from Buffalo to San Francisco were full of the doings of Calamity Jane," the article said. Then, nearly as suddenly as the outburst had broken upon the scene, news of Calamity's activities fell silent, causing some speculation that "possibly Calamity had changed her abode from earthly quarters to the ethereal regions." Others assumed more simply that she had run afoul of an unsympathetic judge in some distant precinct. Neither of these assumptions proved correct. Though Martha remained in South Dakota for nearly six months, she had always intended upon returning to Montana as soon as she was financially able to do so.

Years later, Pierre resident Charles Fales recalled that Martha Jane had arrived wearing "feminine attire—long skirt, white waist and a monstrous flowered hat—then prevailing styles in the east." Pierre photographer R. H. Kelly preserved her image for posterity. But her fashion-plate appearance did little to hide her obvious poverty and failing health. G. H. Grebe recalled her stealing a bottle of whiskey from a local bar and, later, being incapacitated with several broken ribs.

Still, she was Calamity Jane; so the townspeople flowered her with food, clothes, and firewood to see her through the winter. I. N. Walker, then a schoolgirl in Pierre, recounted how Martha took up residence "in an old shack down near the river bottom where the poorer people lived."

Usually, Walker recalled, Martha wore "an old pink gown" around town. She thought Martha, when "properly dressed," looked youngish for her age, around forty. Walker felt that Martha was ill at ease around other women, who mingled with her only when they needed her skills in washing clothes or doctoring the ill. Homesteader Fred L. Fairchild recalled seeing Martha in the Northwestern railroad freight office, coaxing the agent to release her bedstead, mattress, and chairs without paying the overdue freight charges on them.

Martha's tour of South Dakota may have lasted longer than intended by mere geography. There was no railroad bridge crossing the wild Missouri at Pierre; so to get across, she would have had to travel east and then north before finally reaching Montana. Not only that, but severe winter storms meant bad spring floods, halting railroad traffic several times during early 1902.

According to the *Sioux Falls Argus Leader*, Calam divided her time in South Dakota between Pierre, Huron, and Aberdeen, traveling by train and riding in the smoking cars "where the smoke is the thickest and the drinks are passed there most frequently." The newspaper article noted that Martha could "swear oftener and use more blood-curdling oaths in rapid firing order than any other heavyweight of her class."

When an Aberdeen reporter learned of Martha's presence on March 14, he noted that she "gave none of the exciting exhibitions of recklessness which are said to have characterized her visits" throughout her life. Quite the contrary, "She remained quietly at a hotel except during a short time she spent drinking and smoking in a saloon." Yet even then, she managed to attract attention, since it was unusual to see a "nice" woman in a bar. The Aberdeen reporter described Martha as looking so old and tired that she was not likely "to do much more riding on the range clad in buckskin as a man nor participate in many more of the dare-devil escapades which are credited to her."

Martha left Aberdeen on the westbound train and headed east to Evarts, a popular shipping point for cattle along the Missouri River. Ben Arnold, a long-time acquaintance from Virginia City, recalled not recognizing her at first, since she "was old and haggard beyond her years," But after asking a few questions and calling her Jane Somers, referring to the last name of one of Martha's earlier male cohorts, he was convinced. Arnold said that she "carried photographs of herself dressed in buckskin costume, which she sold." He added that many of those she met "made small purchases and refused to take change, as they considered her a fit object of charity."

Although several South Dakota newspapers reported Martha wandering around the eastern part of the state, the Glasgow, Montana, newspaper on March 22 claimed that Calamity Jane was there. With the Glasgow woman was a "girl of about four years." But since no record of Martha at Glasgow or Great Falls exists, let alone carting a four-year-old along with her, it's unlikely that the woman in question was the real Calamity Jane. More likely she was one of dozens of "imposters" who had sprung up around the West, taking the name of the famed western heroine.

Between the following March and April, Calamity was no doubt on the move. She arrived in Huron, South Dakota, on April 8. As the local paper announced, "'Calamity Jane,' of more or less early day fame at Pierre and in the Black Hills country, from '76 to '83, now owner of valuable cattle ranch interests in Montana and the northern Hills country, is in the city." At least the reporter got the "in the city" part correct. Holland (Holly) Wheeler, who owned the pharmacy and general store, recalled Martha's visit to Huron. Calamity had appropriated a boxcar along the railroad tracks where she was staying with a family with five children, "all sick with the flu." Martha stopped by his store to pick up some medicine for them. According to Wheeler, Martha seldom drank, although she "was known to have an occasional cigar and hang out with farmers talking about crops in the saloon."

After a brief stay in Huron and some other local towns, Martha reappeared in Aberdeen that April. "She spent one day here," a reporter said, "and when it became known that she was in town there was much curiosity to see her, and not a few did call upon her." Martha, still upset about having been used by Josephine Brake and the Pan-American Exposition, told the locals she had been "badly cheated" by the "so-called charitable woman" who had whisked her off to Buffalo with faded promises. And then, never being one to let a crowd get away, Martha spun a new yarn about Wild Bill Hickok and his murderer, Jack McCall. She and Bill had decided to get married prior to his being shot, she said. And after he had been killed, she went after the murdering cur, Jack McCall. And she caught him, turned him over to the law, and witnessed him hang in Yankton. Among her most attentive audience members was an old-timer whom Calamity had known thirty years earlier.

"She recognized him in an instant and expressed much pleasure in seeing him again," the newspaper said. The man verified Jane's story, adding that he, too, had witnessed McCall's hanging outside the jail.

Even with the man's heartfelt substantiation, most of the townsfolk found Jane's accounts little more than entertaining. One such skeptic, interviewed by the *Sioux Falls Press*, threw cold water on everything Martha and the old-timer had said. He was quoted as saying that Hickok never had a serious relationship with Martha and that the hanging of McCall did not occur in the Yankton jail yard but rather in the school section two miles north of Yankton. Furthermore, he continued, Martha was not present at the event. The man concluded that, were Wild Bill still alive, the Aberdeen old-timer "might have time to drop to his knees and pray, but he would have to hurry." The article concluded that the "facts" contained within Jane's latest pronouncements were "doleful enough in any case."

Not long after, Martha—who had most likely stopped over in Aberdeen since it was the railway connection between it and Livingston, Montana—left South Dakota, with a layover at Oakes, North Dakota, the railroad's connecting point between the northern and southern parts of the territory. When approached for an interview by a reporter with the *Oakes Republican*, the newspaperman found Martha "not in a condition suitable for an interview." Apparently, she had spent nearly thirty dollars in an Aberdeen saloon the day before and was "still showing the effects." Regardless, Jane was none too hung over to offer to buy the reporter a drink at the local saloon, which he politely refused. Jane looked him squarely in the eye and said that Oakes was "not the town" she thought it was. The article that the paper printed the next day alleged that, except for breakfast at the hotel, Jane spent the entire day in the men's waiting room in the depot, smoking a cigar, before boarding the train for Jamestown at midnight.

But not even that documented story went unchallenged. The James-town newspapers had quite a different, more dramatic take on what had actually happened in Oakes. In the Jamestown accounts, Martha was drinking in an Oakes saloon when "some of the boys" decided to "have a little fun with the 'old woman.'" Martha took in their catcalls and deroga-tory comments for as long as she could before she "pulled out a shootin' iron and the music began." When she was finished "making them dance," one man tried to escape, but she picked up a billiard ball and hurled it at him, bouncing it off his head. The article said she called out to the man that "she would tell him when school was out and he could go." The report also said that, in retrospect, Martha "said she enjoyed society in Oakes very much." The only concession from the *Oakes Republican* that the story was true was a thinly veiled reference to a man named "Mack"—perhaps one of the "boys" involved in the incident?—whom the paper said had "not forgotten his contact with Calamity Jane."

The story of Calamity Jane's prowess with her six-guns garnered nationwide attention, although in predictably less-than-objective fashion. The *New York World* reported:

> *She was on her way from Jamestown, N.D., to Livingston, Mont., when her birthday called for a proper celebration. This was in the cow town of Oakes. She drank much and in one saloon the cowboys began to chaff her.*
>
> *Calamity Jane smiled grimly and asked everyone up to the bar. They howled. Two revolvers suddenly appeared in the woman's hands. She can "draw" as quick as any man who ever lived.*
>
> *"Dance, you tenderfeet, dance!" she commanded grimly, and she fired a few shots by way of emphasis.*
>
> *They danced, and with much vigor. They did other things that she commanded. Calamity Jane is not a person to be trifled with. The manner in which she shut up that saloon was powerfully convincing.*

When a reporter from the *New York World* asked William F. Cody about events in Oakes that day, he "smiled sadly," recalling how "none of us on the frontier ever met any one like her." Calamity was the epitome, the ultimate example of the "old frontier types," he continued. He added that "there is no more frontier any more and never will be again, and that is why we like to look back, and why the few that remain of the old-timers we marched with and fought with have a warm place in our affections, whatever or wherever they may be." Calamity was simply being Calamity, he concluded, "true to herself and the old days."

Martha's stop in Jamestown, the next jumping-off point down the railroad line, introduced her to yet another reporter, this one for the *Daily Capital*. In Martha, the scribe discovered a woman "very willing to talk of herself and her checkered career." She told him she lived in Livingston and made a life for herself by selling "curios and such" to tourists. "Sometimes she wears a buckskin suit . . . and people from the east think she is a 'b-a-d' woman with a big B," he said. But he himself witnessed "only a plain, medium sized woman with an unquenchable thirst" who enjoyed the public's attention. Another Jamestown reporter noted that, although Martha claimed to have a ranch in Montana, she "dressed in ordinary clothing of a woman not possessed of any great amount of money."

An article in the *Jamestown Daily Alert* described Martha upon her arrival as not feeling well. Still, a reporter noted her eyes being "as keen as ever." Martha told reporters she had spent the winter in Pierre with broken ribs. And then, in a voice reminiscent of Cody, she lamented the passing of an era: "Pierre is getting pretty tame. . . . All the west is getting tame nowadays—so different from what it was when I first came through this country."

As Martha continued working her way back to Montana, she stopped off several more times, including at tiny Mandan, North Dakota. The *Mandan Pioneer* wrote on April 18 that she had come "to renew acquaintance with old timers with whom she was a familiar character in times when things were wild and wooly." Typical of the Calam yesteryear, she "proceeded to do things up brown as soon as she arrived and those who did not know of her presence in this vicinity were soon made aware of it."

After leaving Mandan, she landed next in Dickinson where she somehow appropriated "a jug of beautiful proportions and board[ed] for a time at Hotel de Sheriff Goodall."

Finally, after nine months away from home, Martha returned to Montana. The *Billings Daily Gazette*, on April 16, 1902, wrote that Martha, after having been in the "effete and pampered East," had come to the conclusion that "only Montana and its snowcapped mountains and ozone laden prairies can appease her longings for nature, pure and untrammeled," adding that "among the first to be made aware of her return were the saloonmen. She called on a number of them."

Another informant, in what was surely an embellished reminiscence, said that the moment Calamity stepped off the train and onto the platform, "she kicked off those high-heeled shoes about twenty feet in the air. 'God damn 'em,' she hollered, 'I could not live with 'em any longer.'"

Naturally, on her first night back home for the better part of a year, Martha couldn't wait to celebrate with old friends and new and proceeded to tear up the town until a "cruel hearted policeman" arrested her on charges of being drunk and disorderly. After spending a night sleeping it off, she was released. But it was clear from anyone who saw her that, as the Billings paper observed: "Her pride has been wounded and she finds herself disgraced." It had been anything *but* the homecoming welcome she had anticipated and longed to enjoin.

The paper's editor, though, remained unmoved. "Hard as it must seem to her, 'Calamity Jane' is learning that the old west, the west with which her name is linked, has been forced to give way to the west as the tenderfoot would have it." He went on to say that she would need to learn that "the freedom and ease of manners that prevailed in those 'good old days' are gone and conformity to accepted customs is now expected from everybody."

Shortly after the editorializing in the Billings paper, Martha hopped a train for Livingston. The poem announcing her return in the April 24 issue of the *Livingston Post* was similarly caustic.

Calamity Jane is home again from her wanderings far and wide;
She longs no more for the eastern shore and
the surge of the rushing tide;
Back to the hills of her stamping ground she has come to settle down,
Leaving the glare of the hated east for the mountains' restful brown....

Like the prodigal son she sings a song, a song of troubled verse,
With a drink and a dirge, a curse and a prayer,
a cow horse and a hearse.
The fatted calf was dressed for me, she sings in mournful strain,
But the husks have a greater zest for me, and I'm off for my stys again."

Ignoring the remarks, Martha ascended into the small communities ringing Yellowstone Park, where she encountered fewer interruptions from law officers and an increasingly unsympathetic press. By May she was in Horr, after which she moved on to Gardiner at the Park's northern entrance. "Calamity Jane, the notorious, drifted into Gardiner last week," the newspaper said, pointing out that she had "emphasized her arrival in a manner peculiarly her own, and satisfied the average citizen that she was the original and genuine."

While Martha was in Gardiner, a small-time thief named Richard Lee "performed the unmitigated, nervy and inhuman act of 'rolling' Calamity Jane," reported the Livingston paper. According to one of Martha's friends, Lee had stolen from her the ring she claimed Wild Bill Hickok had given her. She described its shape being "like a striking rattlesnake with several complete coils around the finger." Martha swore out a complaint to the sheriff, who located the ring soon after and placed Lee under arrest. But when the time arrived for Lee's arraignment, Martha failed to appear in court, "and as there was no evidence against the defendant he was discharged."

Meanwhile, Martha returned to her "shack" in Gardiner. From there, she continued selling her autobiography to park tourists. But in late May, she suffered some sort of serious illness. At the county's expense, she was whisked back to Livingston, where plans had been made to place her in the Park County Poor Farm until she recovered. But Martha, having suffered such an indignity once before in her life, steadfastly refused to be admitted. Deciding Livingston was no longer the place for her, "she borrowed enough money to buy a few drinks of whisky and a ticket to Lombard," the newspaper said. The county commissioners wanted no responsibility in the matter and announced they would "place no obstacle in her way if she wants to leave the county."

Regardless of her desire to go, Calamity—off on one last spree before leaving town—missed the train. Dousing herself in spirits, she hit one saloon after another until she "had a jag aboard that would have taxed the capacity of an elephant, not to speak of a woman who is now cavorting around in the horizon of her seventieth sunrise," according to the paper. The editor's "guesstimation" of Calamity's age attests to the hard life she had lived: He overestimated it by nearly a quarter of a century.

When the police finally stumbled upon Martha in an intoxicated stupor sleeping it off on a bench in front of the Albemarle Hotel, they arrested her. The newspaper, not about to miss such an opportunity, announced she "was engaged in her old time occupation of playing checkers on a window grate at the county jail."

Martha was released the next day after a promise once again to leave town. Two weeks later, she resurfaced, this time in Lewistown. Carrying on as if she had only recently arrived from her New York escapades, she expressed "no use for the type of civilization encountered in the east." To prove it, she spent the next week celebrating her return "in true western style."

The following week, Martha hopped a stage from Lewistown to nearby Kendall. She "insisted on a seat beside Johnney Harvey on the front boot," the Lewistown paper reported, and the driver had everything to do to keep her from grabbing the reins. "Johnney had to do some tall talking to keep the ribbons," the article said. Along the way, Martha visited the saloon on a stopover at the Spring Creek station, where she spent the rest of the afternoon before completing her trip on the next stage. She apparently remained in the Kendall-Lewistown area for the remainder of the summer. By November, though, records show her returning to Red Lodge near Yellowstone Park. "The famous female scout, Calamity Jane, arrived in the city last Saturday," the *Red Lodge Picket* said, "and for the past week has been renewing acquaintances with the friends of early days over the flowing bowl." When she left Red Lodge on the train for Billings, Martha told several people that she was "not in the best of health." A Billings reporter wrote that he thought Martha's New York experiences had "just about soured her on the human race."

As Martha's health continued to deteriorate, Josephine Brake—by then relocated to Chicago—kept pressuring the federal government for a pension for her, insisting that her role as an army scout entitled her to the funds. Some newspapers in the northern plains states agreed, filling their pages with enjoinders for the "Calamity Jane Fund." Lewistown's *Fergus County Argus* suggested that Brake's efforts needed the support of people's petitions and that she "would receive a hundred thousand signatures west of the Missouri river" alone. The paper went on to say it believed Montana's congressional representatives should "render what aid they could in that direction." In fact, the paper's editor suggested, if constitutional, "a small appropriation" for Martha should be awarded by the state legislators. After all, she had aided her country when called upon; now it was the country's turn to reciprocate. He reminded his readers that Martha "was as brave and intrepid as any of the great Custer's troopers." And, sure enough, when Martha next visited Lewistown, people "stopped in crowds to gaze upon her" and cheer, he said. For them, she revived memories of "the stirring events in which she was a prominent figure."

But not everyone favored granting Martha a government stipend. While those editors who were overwhelmed by Calamity Jane's heroic legend lobbied on her behalf, opponents emphasized her prodigious faults. One such paper, the *Lewistown Democrat*, said it was "an open question as to whether or not this frolicsome lady" deserved any financial consideration at all. The editor opined that Martha had already received more than her fair share of largesse. She had enjoyed "unbounded freedom in her exploitation of those peculiar gifts which distinguish her from the average woman," he said, not to mention "the perpetuation of her name in the temples of historical fame." He concluded that she had had gifts and money lavished upon her throughout her adult life "by those who looked upon her as a wild west heroine." The editor concluded that he simply couldn't justify her receiving more.

The move to sign the petition grew. Among those signees, according to the Billings paper, were people "of influence and wealth." But the government by then had rejected the notion of a subsidy for Martha because no records existed to prove that she ever performed military service. The petitions asked for the government to reverse its decision. No one, though, wanted Martha to receive an unregulated stipend, recognizing that doing so would be courting disaster: She simply would have spent it all on alcohol and fast living. One reporter spelled it out: "It is pitiable to see the old girl now on one of her twisters. . . . She has worn ragged holes in her credit in every saloon from Glendive to Kalispell."

As a proposed solution, pension advocates suggested that Martha be assigned "a guardian, just as if she were a child" and have funds doled out "only at such times as she is in actual want and when she guarantees that she will not spend it over the bar treating every sheep herder she meets." The problem, as one petitioner commented, was that "you might as well try to make a pet out of a timber wolf. She has been footloose all her life, and the quickest way to break her heart would be to take away her peculiar and eccentric ideas of liberty."

The petitioners, in time, lost ground to the "realists," who increasingly viewed Martha as a burden on society and a relic from the Wild West's past. Her allure lay more in her legendary image than in reality. Martha, undoubtedly following the controversy if only at a discreet distance, must have been crushed. She viewed herself as the *reality* of the Old West, not merely an *image* of it. She was the one and only Calamity Jane, the celebrity who had kept the wags and the newspapers rolling in stories of gold for the past thirty years. She and she alone had helped easterners come to terms with just how difficult and challenging life in the West really was. She was, in effect, the West's first and only real female celebrity.

No stronger battle over the legacy of a living legend had ever been fought. And perhaps none ever would be. At least not until Martha's death, when all the issues would resurface, and all the claims and counterclaims for immortality and historical relevance were revisited.

But before that could come to pass, Martha, like William James Hickok before her, had one last hand to play. And, as she would have said herself, it was a doozy.

CHAPTER FOURTEEN

Calamity's Last Ride

One time we were talking of death and decorating of graves. Jane spoke up and said, 'I don't know anybody who would even plant a cactus on my grave.' I promised her then that if I outlived her I would see that her grave was taken care of, and she sleeps today beneath a vase and gravestone I placed there.

—DORA DUFRAN, *LOW DOWN ON CALAMITY JANE*

"JANE ON THE WARPATH," DECLARED THE BILLINGS NEWSPAPER ON November 21, 1902. The article that followed read that, for no apparent reason "save that suggested by a mind more or less disordered by too free indulgence in her favorite tipple," Martha attacked a local female store clerk with a hatchet. Brandishing the weapon over her head, she threatened to slice the woman into bits. Although the reporter thought Martha might have been joking, the female clerk was not amused. After another salesperson disarmed Calamity and ushered her out of the store, the male offered to call the sheriff, but the victim refused to file a formal complaint. But Martha, being Martha, got involved in another melee the following morning and was arrested. The reporter on the scene wrote that the judge would probably sentence her to a stay in the county jail until she's had sufficient time "to get the liquor out of her system."

The two incidents were not peculiar. The residents of Billings had observed Martha growing increasingly abusive toward the townsfolk for several weeks.

"The sad truth of the matter is," a reporter wrote in the *Billings Times* on November 25, "that Jane has been drinking quite freely of late" despite a vow of abstinence she had made earlier that summer. When the fall political campaign swung into high gear, so did Calamity. By the time she boarded the Republican Party's special train to Columbus—no doubt for the free drinks and camaraderie—she had already gotten "a good sized jag" on. She also drank heavily in Laurel and Red Lodge before returning to Billings. The paper noted that she had been imbibing heavily ever since, with some of her best and oldest friends expressing fear that "age and strong drink" had affected her mind.

After the second disruption in two days, the judge proved the newsman's report accurate by giving Calamity sixty days in jail in the hopes that she would use her "time to recruit up, as she is in a bad way physically." But Martha didn't serve the full sentence. Complaining of sickness, she was allowed to see a physician who diagnosed her with severe rheumatism and admitted her to the hospital. As a Billings reporter commented, Calamity Jane, having survived "all kinds of enemies, from Indians to sutlershop whiskey," was finally "compelled to lower her colors to a foe as silent as he is merciless—disease."

Once she had sobered up and returned to good health, Martha was released from the hospital and forgiven her jail sentence. But demon whiskey had become a foe far worse than mere mortal disease, and she quickly returned to her drinking, falling into a condition "which those addicted to the use of the language of the street would designate as 'jagged,' but which a lady of her own refinement would probably describe as 'overcome.'" Not particularly anxious to experience another round of the community's hospitality, she told a reporter that Billings "had become too much of a tenderfoot town." She decided to return to the Black Hills, "where," the reporter wrote, "she had friends and ... would be appreciated for her real worth." Living up to her word, Martha boarded the Burlington on December 12 and left Montana forever.

But the "noted female character" got only as far as Sheridan, Wyoming, before she once more "loaded up on whiskey and remained drunk for several days," the Billings newspaper learned. The good folks of Sheridan were well acquainted with Calamity's reputation for causing a ruckus; so, when she registered at a local hotel, the editor of the *Sheridan Post* wrote only partly tongue in cheek, "The management of the hostelry are polishing up their guns and imploring the marshal for protection." It's likely that the townsfolk of Sheridan were relieved when Martha resumed her trip to the Black Hills. As she boarded the train, she was carrying only a small bag, according to Burlington line conductor Dick Nelson. Seating herself in the men's smoking car, he relayed later that she was "poorly dressed, dirty and unkempt, and down in the dumps." When the conductor came by to collect her ticket, she claimed that friends had purchased one for her but that she had lost it. When her fellow passengers learned who she was, they took up a collection, paid her fare, and gave her some cash for expenses. Following a brief stopover in Custer, the train continued on into Deadwood.

Understandably, the press went crazy with the news. Calamity, after all, was their adopted angel. "Calamity Jane Returns," the *Deadwood Evening Independent* announced on December 15. The reporter, who referred to her as "the leading western scout," said old-timers remembered her with gratitude, for they were "never turned from her door hungry as long as she had food." The article went on to say that Martha was wearing a brown derby and that her face showed "more wrinkles" than previously, but he also lauded her "noticeably slender figure," a compliment that must have turned the head even of Martha. Regardless, the story went on, she was "the same Jane as of old." A writer for *the Deadwood Pioneer-Times* wasn't quite so laudatory, saying that "age is telling on her, and her hair is becoming streaked with gray . . . and she is not the same vivacious Jane of years agone." Martha informed the reporters that after she visited "old friends," she might return to Montana.

As had become her habit, Martha peppered her stay in Deadwood with visits to several neighboring communities. Each town's local newspaper duly noted her arrival and departure. "Mrs. Burke, alias 'Calamity Jane,' was a passenger on last evening's outgoing train, after looking over the city for several days," the *Deadwood Evening Independent* reported on December 19. She returned on Christmas Day "to spend a few of the holidays in her favorite resorts." And, apparently, pursuing one of her favorite pastimes. A dispatch from Cheyenne on January 7 to the

Denver Post declared that Martha was again "on the rampage." That came as something of a surprise to local journalists who, for some reason, had assumed Martha had acquired a new aura of respectability upon returning from New York.

But she hadn't. And times change, even in Deadwood. So, even though "the public had almost forgotten her when she broke loose in celebration of the glad Christmastide," according to one newspaper report, such behavior was no longer endurable in communities of polite society. The outcome was inevitable: "Jane finds herself in the lock-up, where she is now, and scheduled among the plain drunk."

A few weeks later, Calamity had left Deadwood for the cow town of Belle Fourche, set just north of the Black Hills. The *Belle Fourche Bee* on January 15 reported that Calamity had decided to live there permanently. "She says she is tired of travelling and desires to locate somewhere, where she can lead a quiet life, earn her living in an honorable manner and spend the balance of her days in peace and quiet." Arriving with Calamity, according to the paper, was her daughter, Jessie. The reason for her daughter's visit to Belle Fourche wasn't clear. But the papers reported that Martha was in search of a job, saying that she was capable of "washing, cooking or nursing" and emphasized her desire to "support herself and daughter in a proper manner." Martha's talents as a nurse were widely known and prompted special mention by the article's author. "When others passed by on the other side, she, of her own accord, visited the sick and took care of them."

Belle Fourche, a shipping embarkation for cattle, was still a rough-and-tumble cow town that reminded Calamity "of old times, then getting pretty tame in other places," according to friend and brothel madam Doris DuFran. Martha had worked for DuFran at various times as a cook and laundress. According to DuFran, she arrived carting everything she owned "in a dilapidated old suit case." Inside were her buckskin outfit, a couple of calico dresses, and some "unmentionables." Following the local paper's lead, DuFran praised Martha for her "many hundreds of deeds of kindness" performed without ever thought for pay. Growing up without any proper guidance and in an era of wide-open lawlessness, Martha was "a product of the wild and wooly west . . . not immoral; but unmoral."

A long-time Belle Fourche resident, Samuel G. Mortimer, recalled the day Martha stopped at his hardware store. After a customer had addressed him by name, Calamity turned and asked if he was related to the George Mortimer she had known in Montana. He said George, since deceased, had been his father. Martha threw her arms around him as if a long lost relative and told him she was going to "do laundry work for the girls in the Red Light District." When he asked how he could help, she told him she would need certain supplies and equipment: washtubs, a flatiron, soap, starch, laundry clips, and other things. He rounded them up for her, and she promised to make payments from her wages, a promise she lived up to. *Until* she fell off the wagon.

Mortimer later acknowledged, "When she was 'in her cups,' she was pretty much of a nuisance ... and swore like a trooper." Unfortunately, her all-too-many drinking sessions usually left her penniless and repentant. Then she'd come in and ask Mortimer for "a small loan" to buy food and other necessities. In the end, she had managed to repay all of her bills except for three dollars still due when she died.

Dora DuFran also recounted Martha's drinking sprees. Calamity had managed to remain sober for nearly six weeks when "the old urge overcame her good resolutions," the madam recalled. The day after payday, DuFran knew Martha had fallen off the wagon when she heard Calamity's "wild howls" off in the distance. After celebrating for the better part of a week, Martha returned to work.

During her revelries, DuFran recalled, Martha wore "her buckskin suit, high-heeled boots and Stetson hat, a wide ammunition belt and two forty-fours, holstered at each side." Although Martha never shot anyone, she certainly scared enough people half to death merely by drawing her guns "when in a peevish fit." However, she was easily placated: It took only an apology and the offer of a drink or two to make her "forget any differences in a moment."

According to DuFran, Martha preferred hard liquor to beer. It worked quicker and cost only a little more. Whenever she bellied up to the bar to order a drink, she always exclaimed, "Give me a shot of booze and slop her over the brim." She'd continue drinking until, as DuFran called it, she reached the "howling stage." Since "nothing could quell the howling completely," it fell to one of her friends to "escort her home with a quart of whiskey hugged to her breast to act as a night cap and put her to sleep." Such drunken revelry often went on for days. Unless, of course, she learned of someone who was sick. Then she'd stop drinking in an instant and be hard at work within the day. DuFran, a keen Calamity observer, noted that "about six weeks was her sober limit."

One of Martha's drinking sprees in Belle Fourche ended prematurely after some of her cowboy buddies played a practical joke on her. While Martha snored off her most recent drunk, the men powdered her face with charcoal dust. The following morning, Martha pulled herself out of bed and wandered over to the post office. The clerk, thinking she was a masked robber, promptly fainted. The postmaster scolded Martha so severely that she decided to sober up, said DuFran, and "peace came once more to the city."

A month later, according to the *Belle Fourche Bee*, Martha "pulled out for a ranch," where she had "obtained employment for the season." Martha told a reporter she had been working as a cook at "a Belle Fourche hotel" but found the work too hard for her at her age. That may well have been true because, before heading to the ranch, she stopped off at Hot Springs, some hundred miles south of Belle Fourche, where she gave an interview to the *Hot Springs Weekly Star*, saying she had come to visit old friends. The town of Hot Springs was noted for its healthful baths, and the paper confirmed that Martha had spent "a few weeks for her health" there—although, rather than reporting fact, the article was probably conjecturing that she wouldn't have gone there for any other reason *but* her health.

Yet, even while recuperating, Calam couldn't give up her liquor. John Stanley, the future editor of the *Lead Daily Call*, recalled being in Hot Springs carrying some official documents to the courthouse when he learned that Calamity Jane was drinking at the Bodega Saloon. When Stanley entered the saloon and introduced himself, Martha pretended they had met before. When Stanley let down his guard, she grabbed his document satchel and refused to return it until he agreed to buy drinks for the house.

A few days later, Martha left for Rapid City to the north, where she planned to attend the annual carnival. The *Rapid City Daily Journal* called her visit "particularly fortunate," adding that she was "one of the most widely celebrated characters in the west" and would certainly add flair to their April festivities. But Calamity's poor health continued to plague her, and in time she grew ill enough to merit calling a doctor. Sometime after examining her, Dr. R. J. Jackson commented that, when Martha had come to see him, she was in "bad shape" and "beyond help," so he gave her "some harmless medicine." Once she began feeling better again, Martha returned to Deadwood, telling the Rapid City reporter that she would come back to town in time for the celebrations.

Meanwhile, the Rapid City newspaper ran ads promoting the biggest and best "eleventh annual meeting of the Western South Dakota Stockgrowers' Association" along with the "carnival of western sports," promising to be the "Biggest Event of Years." The paper fueled the frenzy, saying the town had been "decorated from stem to stern and everybody was out for a good time." The events included barrel racing, square dances, concerts, political speeches, and even a parade—everything, in fact, except Martha. The elusive Ms. Cannary disappeared from the radar for a time, showing up next in mid-June in Sundance, Wyoming. Her trip there from Aladdin once again made the front page of the local newspaper.

Calamity Jane was visiting in Sundance last week for the first time in the history of the town. She rode into town on the hack from Aladdin and the people became very much interested as soon as they found who the visitor was. There were a few who had known her in the early days and to these the rest looked for verification as to the genuineness of Calamity. George Berghofer, one of the pioneers of '76, declared it was she and the pioneer woman was then given a warm reception.

She has been in the Hills several months this trip, passing from one camp to another, and subsisting on the bounty of her pioneers friends and it was but natural that she should include Sundance in her itinerary. Riding across from Aladdin in the hack, when she met a man she would ask him for a drink of whiskey or a smoke. She passed two young fellows herding horses. They were sitting on the ground playing cards. "High, low Jack and the game," she shouted. "Got a bottle?" They declared they had no bottle. Then she asked for a smoke.

They had no smoking, and she asked for a chew. One of them produced a plug of Climax and she took a chew that would make a Kentuckian ashamed of himself. Several times on the way to Sundance she accosted people in this way and the driver, a young fellow seventeen years old, had a novel experience to relate afterwards.

A Sundance furniture-store owner, William R. Fox, recalled Calamity as an everyday woman more closely resembling someone of eighty years of age than one of forty-seven. "Dressed in a dark-colored garment of poor material; her stringy gray hair twisted into a careless knot at the nape of her neck; her skin wrinkled and sallow, she was indeed an object of pity," Fox said. His impression was that she believed she was entitled to handouts because of who she was. Martha "had no scruples about asking for anything she wanted." She put up in a vacant room in the American House Hotel, which Fox had decorated for her using goods from his store. Other locals responded to her visit by bringing groceries, a cook stove, and even spending money. The seven saloons in town agreed to furnish her with "whiskey all the time she lived there." Fox recalled her being "groggy with liquor most of the time." He said she had made his store her "loafing place," telling her exaggerated tales of life on the frontier so often that he finally began tuning her out. He said that all of the stories were the same tall tales he'd heard about her for years. Fox added that Martha told him she was in town in search of her husband, who she said had arrived sometime earlier. But Fox didn't believe it because "she had claimed so many different men as her husbands."

Barbara Henderson Fox, at the time only a child, recalled watching Martha strut down the street with a "five pound lard pail full of foaming beer." Unlike William, Barbara found Martha captivating, if somewhat intimidating, admiring the "careless grace" of the tall, thin, good-looking woman who had the courage to ignore all the town wags. "The fact that she would have nothing to do with the women of the town added to her attractiveness." Martha justified Barbara's faith in her when she went out of her way to tend to an old freighter on his last legs. After he had died, Barbara recalled Martha sitting beside his body all night "while she drank quantities of beer and wept copiously."

Crying for a stranger was not in Martha's nature. Crying for a human being meeting a premature end to his life was. Cut short by the cruelness of Death, the man's plight had touched her to her soul. Ironically, she bonded with his spirit only after he had passed.

Or perhaps it was Martha's unwillingness to admit that there was nothing she couldn't face, nothing she couldn't do on earth. Renowned so widely for her nurturing and nursing skills, perhaps she believed herself to be impervious to the ravages wreaked by failure. She had never recognized it in her own life, although she could easily have done so time and again. Failure as a child to protect her brother Cilus from a tyrannical father; failure to move her mother to redemption; inability to prevent her parents' premature deaths and the abandonment of their children to the winds. Failure, even, to have been born female in a world that valued males far more.

Regardless, it was clear that the man's death took its toll on her. Several weeks later, without a word to anyone, she left town, drifting once again back through the various communities of the Black Hills.

Dora DuFran, in her booklet, *Low Down on Calamity Jane*, recalled one "last big spree" in Belle Fourche that summer. When DuFran wrote about Calamity in 1932, she could "still remember the wild yells" Martha made "as she topped the hill," riding behind a cowboy heading for Spearfish, where Martha set off on a three-day spree before she "caught a ride to Deadwood on the Spearfish stage." Confirming DuFran's recollection, the Spearfish newspaper on July 8 reported that "Calamity Jane, the one and only, really and gracious Calamity, blew in from Belle Fourche Monday and is telling her old Spearfish friends what she thinks of them." From there, Martha traveled on to visit Lead, where the local constables kindly invited her "to take a hike," according to the newspaper, and "she compromised by taking the first train she could catch that was headed for Deadwood."

Martha's timing couldn't have been better. The National Editorial Association had recently selected Deadwood as a "point of interest," and the town fathers couldn't have been more proud. The editor of the *Deadwood Pioneer-Times* devoted nearly two columns of space in the July 12, 1903, paper, calling attention to the town's schools, churches, and industries. His editorial, though, warned Deadwood to stand down from its "Old West" aura. The visitors "will expect to find the Deadwood of romance of twenty-five years ago," he wrote. Instead, he advised that the tourists be free to discover that "Wild Bill sleeps peacefully in Mount Moriah cemetery." Thanks to him and the men who followed after him, he wrote, "bad men" no longer shoot up the town, and "the county jail and city calaboose are . . . largely ornamental now."

Into this celebration strode Calamity Jane, a living, breathing emissary of the town's frontier past, just as the association of editors came to call. When they received word of the presence of the notorious Calamity Jane, they scrambled to witness her firsthand. A writer for the *Daily Pioneer-Times* wrote later that "she is not as robust nor as picturesque as she was ten or fifteen years ago . . . [but] she possesses all her original traits and characteristics." Noting the visiting editors' fascination with her, the Deadwood paper revised its editorial tone sharply, recalling the city's gold rush days and calling Martha "one of the truly unique characters of the West." About that time, the editor learned that Martha's daughter, Jessie, was married and living in North Dakota with two children. "It seems rather odd to think of Calamity Jane as a grand-mother, but she [Martha] says it is true nevertheless." Interestingly, no evidence exists that Martha was ever blessed with any grandchildren.

After leaving Deadwood, an article in the *Rapid City Daily Journal* reported that the "distinguished, notable and typical plains woman of '76 fame" was once again their guest. Rapid City, it seems, was thrilled at the honor. As one reporter noted, "There is hardly enough rubber now in people's necks it seems to allow them to stretch it far enough to get a good look at Jane."

For no apparent reason other than wanderlust, Martha soon bounced back to Deadwood for what would turn out to be her last visit. There, a liquor-business owner who was also an amateur photographer took a touching photograph of Jane standing aside the grave of Wild Bill Hickok, further cementing the image of the "loving couple" for eternity. John B. Mayo said he had asked Martha to pose graveside for him one day as they rubbed elbows at a saloon in Sundance. Martha said she'd be delighted, indicating she'd be back in Deadwood within the week. When, a week later Mayo and a boarder of his searched Deadwood for her, they discovered her sitting on a keg behind a saloon. Two sheets to the wind, Martha followed the men to the cemetery. Mayo had volunteered to hire a coach to make the arduous trek up to the graveyard, but Martha insisted on walking, saying, "Anytime I can't walk up there to lay a rose on poor Bill's grave, I'll letyuh know it."

As the trail grew progressively steeper, crossing a ravine on the way to the summit, Mayo recalled how he "sweated blood getting Jane across that canyon." She was "woozy, panting, and weaving as she plodded along on the high track, which was nothing but a narrow bridge, and we had our hands full of equipment. I half expected her to take a header off the trestle into the gulch bottom."

But they finally reached their destination—Mount Moriah Cemetery—when Mayo found yet another obstacle in his path. "The grave had an iron rail fence around it, and the gate was locked," he said, "so I decided to take a picture of Jane standing in front of the grave holding the flower that I brought along." But, as Mayo was setting up for the photo, Martha "fell asleep on me—standing up."

After nudging her awake, he handed her an artificial flower to place on the grave as he prepared for the exposure. Martha wasn't amused. "What would poor old Bill think of [me] placing a phony rose on his grave?" Putting aside the flower issue, Mayo ducked beneath the dark cloth to check on his focus when Martha cried out, "What in hell yuh hidin' yer head for?" She had assumed he wanted to have his picture taken with her. "Any damn time I'm too old to have a picture taken with a young whipper-snapper, I'm too old to have any picture taken!"

Realizing that he had come too far to fail, Mayo arranged to stand beside her as his companion snapped the photo. Later, he finally succeeded in getting the shot of her he had envisioned all along—Martha standing alone beside Bill's gravesite.

Mayo wasn't the only photographer to capture Calamity that summer. A man named Charles Haas also photographed her. He had been strolling down the wooden walk with his camera flung over his shoulder in nearby Whitewood when Martha saw him and asked him to take her picture. Haas recalled, "I hopped off this old board sidewalk and took the picture," and then Martha said, "Now how about a couple of drinks?" Haas followed her to Jackson and Gustine's saloon, one of Calamity's favorite haunts. Halfway through their first drink, the photographer decided he wanted a souvenir of his meeting with the one and only western legend.

"The saloon had those tokens that you paid with," he recalled, "and I thought I'd like to keep the token that I paid for her drink with." When Martha noticed him pocketing it, she bristled, demanding an explanation. Haas told her he only wanted a remembrance of her, at which she smiled, nodded her head, and said, "Oh, that's very nice." Haas wore the token on his watch fob for the rest of his life. "Lots of us in Whitewood, and here in Deadwood, too, knew the better side of Calamity," he said.

His photograph depicted an aged, ordinary-looking woman in stark contrast to the romanticized image captured by Mayo at Hickok's grave.

Haas related several other stories about Martha's generous nature, recounting his admiration for her. One was about a young grocery clerk who told him Martha had walked into his store, filled a basket she carried on one arm, and walked out without paying. When the clerk revealed to his boss what had happened, the owner informed him that Martha could have whatever she wanted because she was taking food and supplies for the sick and homeless. Unfortunately, Haas added, Martha "would go to these bawdy houses and dance halls and it was whoopee and soon she was drunk and then, well, things just sort of went haywire with old Calamity."

Martha's illness was apparent from Haas's photograph and supported by the local newspaper, which said she had announced upon arriving in town "that she was going to cash in." But, still, her drinking continued.

Martha was still "fairly heavy with liquor" when she ran into some Burlington railroad men who had assembled on the corner across from the Bodega Bar. Engineer Joe Hilton later recalled someone purposefully setting her off by mentioning Buffalo Bill Cody. She "started to give [Cody] a tongue lashing" because of the way she'd been "stranded in New York and was pretty mad about it." When the party was about to break up, Martha said she planned on going to Terry in the morning. Hilton told her when and from where the train would depart and advised her to be ready. The following day, she was there awaiting the train, right on time.

"We got off the engine where Calamity was and we talked to her for a few minutes and we told her that when we pulled up to where she was, why she could get on," the engineer said, "and that's the last I saw of her." Hilton recalled that she looked hungover and "terrible." Martha rode "on the last car of the ore train, a boxcar converted into a sort of day-car" used mostly by the railroad men. Hilton later recalled he had been the one who "gave Calamity Jane her last ride."

Martha showed up in Terry on July 24, 1903. Not long after, according to the *Terry News-Record*, "the heroine of many a lurid tale of the Black Hills, and whose name is interwoven with the early history of this region as a daring government scout and bull-whacker" was ill. *Seriously* ill. She was taken to a room in the Calloway Hotel where Jane told her visitors that "all my old pards have gone over the divide and I am ready to go too." Later, an acquaintance, H. A. Scheffer, moved Martha Jane to his own establishment and sent for Dr. Richards. When the physician arrived to examine her, Martha put up a fuss. When the doctor became impatient with her, a reporter commented that "she was inclined to assert the old time vindictiveness and her weakened condition alone, kept her from adding another combat to her record."

Martha Jane Cannary, despite the doctor's most heroic efforts, took one last breath, closed her eyes, and died on August 1, 1903, at 5 p.m. The cause of death: "inflammation of the bowels." Her life-long drinking had contributed to her demise. Although she was only forty-seven years of age, she looked, according to some observers, to be ninety.

The Deadwood newspaper reported that Martha had requested W. R. Monkman, editor of the *Terry News-Record*, to retrieve her trunk, which she had left in Spearfish, and deliver it to Lottie Stacey, the Belle Fourche daughter of a Deadwood pioneer. Martha told Monkman, who was among the last people to see Martha before she slipped off into the other world, the information she wanted him to include in her obituary. That information included the existence of Martha's married daughter, living at an undisclosed location in North Dakota. As Martha's death neared, Monkman rode off to Deadwood to engage the support of the

Society of Black Hills Pioneers, a group that for years was prominent in assisting with the funeral arrangements of the area's early settlers. The *Pioneer-Times* soon reported that "F. X. Smith, one of the Pioneers, will go to Terry today to take charge of the remains" for services to be held in Deadwood.

Even though Martha and the highly respected members of the society were never close friends, the old-timers, who included Smith, Jack Gray, and J. W. Allen, remembered "her acts of kindness when there was no other woman in the gulch and when those in distress must have perished but for her thoughtfulness," according to a newspaper account. The Pioneers agreed to give Martha "the best funeral their means [would] command."

Naturally, word of Calamity Jane's demise spread faster than the pox she helped to battle. Some of the details were actually true. One that wasn't involved the nebulous account of some of Deadwood's citizens who learned of the death while drinking together in Mike Russell's saloon. Someone suggested they "give her a big last sendoff." That, of course, called for another round. And by the time the bar was ready to close, they had evolved some elaborate plans for the plainswoman. They planned to spread "word . . . calling on all business houses to close during the services." That left the decision as to where Martha should be buried. The rowdies immediately provided the answer: next to Wild Bill Hickok! "Now Wild Bill had absolutely no use for Jane, but this distinguished self appointed committee decided it would be a good joke on the old boy to make him 'layup' with her for all eternity," the relater of the story said.

The truth is that the decision to bury Martha near Hickok was made during her final days: "At her request," the *Deadwood Pioneer-Times* reported, "the remains will be buried in Mount Moriah Cemetery at Deadwood beside those of William Hickok, 'Wild Bill' her former consort, who was murdered in Deadwood in 1876."

But before Martha could be buried in Deadwood, her body had to be *moved* to Deadwood. So a group of friends loaded her remains onto a wagon for the eight-mile trip from Terry. The driver never lacked for company; several of Martha's friends began the journey with him.

The number increased as the journey progressed until it resembled a small parade. The group made at least one unscheduled stop—and perhaps several—to celebrate Calam's final journey. According to Mrs. John Traul, the group stopped off at several local saloons for hours at a time. Meanwhile, Calamity's body lay unattended in the wagon, which was certainly more appropriate than carting her in with them to the bar.

Meanwhile, in Deadwood, burial preparations had been left to the discretion of C. H. (Charlie) Robinson, the town mortician. He and his father, Henry, worked together in the mortuary. Years after the burial, Charlie recalled that the funeral preparations for Jane weren't the first he'd provided for her. Years earlier a crowd of drunken revelers decided to call the embalmer to the saloon with word that Calamity Jane had passed away. When Robinson arrived, the local prostitutes were all standing in a group, snickering. As the mortician approached the "corpse," he found Martha's torso covered with a sheet, hands folded across her chest, and her face dusted with enough flour "to make a batch of biscuits." Suspecting instantly that something was awry, Robinson asked for a knife to cut into the corpse—just to make sure that Martha was dead. Suddenly, the corpse leaped to its feet, yelling, "Dam you Jack, you ain't going to cut me full of holes. I'll shoot you, if you come near me." Despite having seen through the subterfuge, Robinson was talked into buying the next round of drinks for the house.

When on August 1 Martha's body was brought to Robinson after her *real* death, he announced that Jane's remains would be on display for public viewing "for three days with someone by her side to protect the body from any harm." According to one eyewitness, a guard was placed next to her because "numbers of curious women came to look upon her, and many clipped locks of hair from the head, to the extent of defacing the remains." Eventually, Robinson installed a wire screen over Martha's head to keep her from further mutilation. He was so concerned about maintaining Martha's dignity in her final days on display that he personally watched over her remains. Only later did the town learn that Robinson had donated all of his services to the preparations. It seems he recalled several years earlier when Martha had been the only person to volunteer to care for his younger sister when, in 1878, she was terminally ill with typhoid. Tending for Martha's remains seemed the least he could do in return.

On the day of the funeral, Martha's casket was delivered to the Deadwood Methodist Church, where its pastor, Dr. Charles B. Clark, preached the sermon—this despite the fact that, as reported by the *Deadwood Pioneer-Times*, "Jane had not been a church goer and her life had been characterized by frequent debauches from church ways."

So, the service unfolded on August 4, and the church was packed with spectators and mourners, many of them old settlers who had known, ridden alongside, and bent an elbow with Jane many times before. Martha's casket was nearly hidden from view by the "masses of floral offerings," according to the Deadwood paper. The minister was faced with the task of delivering the eulogy without sounding maudlin—and he did so charitably and honestly, emphasizing Martha's numerous humanitarian acts during Deadwood's earliest years. Echoing popular sentiment, Clark asked, "How often amid the snows of winter did this woman find her way to the lonely cabin of the miner" to help him through his debilitating illness? The minister went on to say that, once the history of the Black Hills was written in the annals of time, "Jane Burke will, in all the deeds which kindness and charity dictated in those early days, be the heroine."

After the eulogy, several hundred persons filed by the coffin to view the woman they had known and lived with, loved and reviled, admired and condemned for decades. The Deadwood band led the funeral procession to Mount Moriah Cemetery, where Martha was interred. Right next to Wild Bill Hickok. According to Mrs. A. M. Workman, a Black Hills resident and one of the funeral attendees, once the ceremony was complete and everyone began filing back to town, someone yelled, "Let's go and have a drink on Calamity!"

Except, just as with Calamity in life, they didn't stop with one. By the time the day was through, most of the men who had attended the funeral had staggered out of the bar, falling-down drunk.

Although no one at the time of Martha's death objected to the location of her interment, Hickok's family and friends later took offense. Lorenzo B. Hickok wrote to Lawrence County officials about the proximity of her grave to that of his brother's. It took the clerk of courts, Sol

Star, to reply that the "records show that a lot was purchased alongside and outside of the lot (fenced) of your Brother's for the burial of Calamity Jane . . . [and] said lot does in no wise conflict or disturb the resting place of J. B."

Another complainant, Captain Jack Crawford, stated publicly several months later that Hickok's name "should in no way be associated with Calamity Jane's," since the two had met only a few weeks before Hickok's assassination. He concluded that news accounts of her final request "to sleep by the side of the man she first loved" were nonsense.

In the days after Martha's funeral, rumors circulated that one man who attended wept uncontrollably. An investigating reporter found that a man named Saunders claimed "that he and Jane passed vows of eternal constancy upon their separation" just before he was sent to prison in Michigan, after which he "came back to the Black Hills to get her, not knowing she was dead."

But none of Deadwood's old-timers could recall the man or any mention of him, so the newspaper flatly condemned him as an imposter.

Although Saunders was the first "fake" to try to take advantage of Calamity Jane's fame, he would not be the last. After the funeral, a local "Hindoo seer" claimed that he had prophesied the time of Martha's death "to within a week." Claiming that he had read her fortune, he said she received word of her upcoming demise with resignation. "I think you're right," she supposedly told him, "because I've felt since coming to the Black Hills this time that I probably wouldn't get away." The seer, who for a price had been predicting the fortunes of various local mining ventures, was exploiting Martha's death for his own well-being.

Regardless, news of the death of Calamity Jane exploded throughout the West. Editors dealt with her controversial reputation in a variety of ways. The Deadwood newspaper commented that Martha Burke, "the 'Calamity Jane' of border fiction," was "one of the most unique feminine characters of the Western frontier" and "died as she had lived, in defiance of all traditions." The reporter then broke into a fanciful tale of her western career:

She was "slender and of a beauty that bewildered the western miners" as a youth in the Montana goldfields. Allowed to run unfettered across the countryside, she became the familiar of freighters, hunters, miners, and trappers. When she joined an expedition to the Black Hills, she took "a step towards a career that few American women have equaled." The reporter repeated the oft-told tales of Martha serving as a scout and messenger for the army, living with Wild Bill in Deadwood in 1876, and capturing Jack McCall after he had murdered Hickok. However, to his credit, he was creative enough to add a new wrinkle to the event when he claimed Martha had not only cornered McCall with a meat cleaver from the butcher shop but also "would have severed his head from his body but for the intervention of bystanders."

But, the scribe added, Martha also displayed feminine qualities, and "constituted doctor, nurse, and cook to many of the miners who became afflicted with smallpox and other diseases." Because of this, he concluded, the true remaining pioneers of the Hills "speak her name almost reverently."

The *Lead Daily Call* exhibited noticeably fewer flowery fantasies in its retelling of Martha's career. While it agreed that the woman had assisted in caring for the sick and dying in an early Deadwood epidemic, it noted that she "was never taken seriously by the people of the Black Hills" except for a brief time when she was suspected of aiding bandits and road agents. Most of the deeds attributed to her, the *Daily Call* explained, were a result of "the doubtful romancers of the east" who "allowed their imagination to run riot."

The newspapers of the day often used obituaries as a primary source of conveying information about a deceased person, while freely exaggerating or adding to the basic facts to satisfy the morbid desires of their readers. Standard practice included adding stories from local sources and persons, previously published accounts, and interviews with people of dubious character who claimed to have known the deceased—or at least known of someone *else* who claimed to have known him! Calamity's death was no exception.

The *New York Times*, as an example, featured her basic obituary but added to it the headline: "Woman Who Became Famous as an Indian Fighter." The article itself read more like a dime novel than a serious obit, claiming that Calamity had once served with Generals Custer and Miles and had become "a carrier of the Government mails in those dangerous times, when men would not venture to make the trip across the prairies." Due to her resultant fame, the *Times* continued, "thousands of tourists went miles out of their way to see her. . . . Speculators fenced in her house and charged an admission fee to tourists." Calamity, had she been alive, no doubt would have approved.

Even the foreign press joined in on the feeding frenzy. In its notice of the famed "Indian fighter's" death, the *London Star* interviewed William F. Cody, then touring in England. Buffalo Bill informed the reporter doing the piece that Martha had never been employed by the government as a scout, although she sometimes accompanied the troops as a "mascot." He added that "whenever she could get hold of any whisky she was pretty sure to paint the town red." Still, not knowing exactly where to draw the line between fantasy and reality—or whether such a line actually existed!—Cody added stories about his "old Pard" Calam that seemed more at home in the pages of a Deadwood Dick pamphlet than in a feature article. In one such story, he alluded to Calamity's frequent skirmishes with Indians, saying, "Jane was always up on the firing line." Then he said her best work wasn't in fighting Indians; it was in helping law officers apprehend desperate criminals, a task at which she excelled!

Cody's name, of course, appealed to hundreds of thousands of readers and lent an air of authenticity to the legendary heroine of the prairie. Newspapers around the world picked up the story and reprinted it, sometimes adding stories of their own as the need to fill space reared its editorial head.

Some papers dug down deeper and discovered an interview with Cody that had been published a year earlier—long before Jane's demise— and published "facts" from that. In that earlier account, Buffalo Bill buffaloed the world with tales of how Jane had first traveled west with her parents to Virginia City, Nevada, instead of to Virginia City, Montana. At the age of ten, he continued, the family was attacked by Indians and Jane got separated from them. Wandering around on her own, she taught herself how to ride and shoot and became the skilled plainswoman she was. "Before she was 20," Cody continued, "General Cook appointed her a scout under me. . . . Her life was pretty lively all the time." He illuminated a frequent subject swirling around Martha Jane: "Though she did not do a man's share of the heavy work, she has gone in places where old frontiersmen were unwilling to trust themselves, and her courage and good-fellowship made her popular with every man in the command." He must have winked when he acknowledged *that*.

Other inaccurate stories made the rounds as well. One biographical account of Calamity's life in an 1896 issue of the *Chicago Daily Inter-Ocean* similarly included several inaccuracies that were also picked up and relayed in many of her obituaries. The egregious falsehood of Martha's involvement in "every lynching bee" in early Deadwood was among the worst. And in the paper's retelling of Jane's own autobiographical entry regarding saving the runaway stage from hostile Indians, it named the driver "Jack McCaul, [who] was wounded by an arrow." When none of the males aboard the coach was brave enough "to take the ribbons," Calamity leaped up onto the boot and drove the stage to "West Birch." After "McCaul" had recovered from his flesh wound, he hunted down and killed Wild Bill Hickok in cold blood. As if that yarn weren't bad enough, it continued with Martha grabbing a butcher's cleaver to capture the assassin. Before long, "McCaul's body was swinging from the limb of a cottonwood tree."

Not to be outdone by the gatekeepers of the Fourth Estate, a number of poets wrangled their works into print to help romanticize the woman's days on earth. Several days after her funeral, on August 20, the *Deadwood Pioneer-Times* published one such poem by George W. Hale.

No more wild oaths, no pistol crack,
No games of death with mountain men;
The broncho and the dear old shack,
I have no further use for them.

Another poem, "Epitaph," written by E. P. Corbin, was published by the same paper three days later, espousing the eternal devotion that existed between Wild Bill Hickok and Calamity Jane:

In spirit land they have met and kissed,
Billing and cooing over all they missed.
Closed for aye, this earthen door,
Man must never open more.
Alas and alack, such love as thine
Wild, unchaste, in constancy almost Divine.

Such remarkably indulgent romanticism pushed the paper's editor over the line. On August 23, he ran a scathing editorial headlined, "Let Them Rest." He argued that the passing of neither Wild Bill nor Calamity Jane was anything more than life and death and that, considering their dubious histories, was mired in duplicity. Since the first thing visitors asked upon landing in Deadwood was the "real scoop" on the pair, the editor declared the topic a "red rag to the editorial bull." Why not emphasize the more positive aspects of the town, he asked. Let Calamity and Wild Bill "rest in their graves. . . . They are dead now and there was nothing in the lives of either with which to make a hero or point a moral."

In support of his comments, the *Pioneer-Times* printed a similarly negative account of Martha Jane's life by M. L. Fox, who eight years earlier had interviewed and supported her. Reaching a different conclusion with the passage of time, Fox credited the dead woman's fame to "eccentric habits and 'penny dreadful' story writers," rather than to any heroic deeds of her own. Although Fox allowed Martha was kindhearted and "ready to nurse the sick or give her last penny to anyone who needed it," she did not, according to the writer, deserve her laudatory reputation. Calamity Jane had never joined the army or served as a scout, and she had never "killed either an Indian or a white man." Rather, she was "an ignorant woman of most unwomanly habits" who tore around the dance hall floors and frequented the saloons. Although she "dressed in the garb of a man, carried revolvers and a knife in her belt and a Winchester rifle," she was unworthy of "any notoriety beyond what I have stated."

What Fox *didn't* say was that Martha never shrank from a fight or a deed that needed to be done. If the legendary plainswoman had to elaborate on some of her life's adventures to drive home to others the depth of her willingness of spirit, all the more understandable. No one calls upon a shrinking violet in his hours of need; everyone calls upon a hero.

Still, notwithstanding the scathing postmortem reviews, a few newspapers defended Martha's life on earth. The *Rapid City Daily Journal*, while confessing that Calamity's fame arose "only because she did so many things unusual for a woman to do," thought the press was being too hard on her. "Calamity drank the wine of life, draining the cup to its dregs," but in the process, she did "many kindly, womanly things," concluding that, "when she stands before the Great Judge she will be on equal footing."

But such laudatory statements were few and far between, particularly in the papers of the northern plains towns. Rapid City's *Black Hills Union* speculated on the reception Martha would likely receive at the gate of St. Peter. In an editorial entitled "The Cup and Its Dregs," the *Union* scoffed at accounts concerning Martha's "charity, her goodness of heart and her glittering career." Instead, the editor insisted, her life "was one of wanton waywardness and debauchery." The *Union*, unsympathetic with those writers and others who ascribed Calamity's flamboyant behavior to her deficient social upbringing, alleged her early years were no better or worse than those of other young women who managed to climb above their deficiencies to lead honorable and even noble lives. Calamity chose to avoid the truly "brave acts" of hard work, education, and respectability. Not even her humanitarianism made up for her shortcomings. After all, the paper argued, "thousands of virtuous girls" risked their lives every day working as nurses in the wards of battlefields of the country, without concern for contagious disease.

What the editor of the *Black Hills Union* failed to consider was that nursing was a purely selfless act on Martha's behalf. It was, unlike the case with thousands of other women, neither her job nor her avocation but rather her big heartedness that forced her to respond to other people's suffering and urgencies.

The editor of the *Union* went on to chastise those whom he considered guilty of whitewashing Calamity Jane's life. "The worst sample of the silly slush being published just now is from the pen of some water-brained ninny by the name of George Walter Hale, of Central."

Objecting to Hale's poem as nothing more than "hero worship," he admonished: "Ask the honest pioneer what Jane was famous for and he will tell you that she was noted for the amount of bad whiskey she could get away with and for being so low and debased that she was fit company only for dogs." Her "noble escort, Wild Bill," he added, was "a good for nothing lout whose handsome person and cleverness at murdering innocent people gained him some dime novel notoriety." The editor railed against "the sort of scum that are held up to our girls and boys as being noble-hearted and heroic men and women whom unavoidable circumstances compelled to adopt the lives they lived. What rank falsehood! What puerile and nauseating stuff!"

What the editor failed to consider was the fact that most American heroes over the years have been glorified more by the pen than by the sword. Only the passage of time can tell the true depth of a person's inner spirit and outermost action. The tarnished episodes of a hero's life have long since been forgiven and forgotten, as have those of Jane. The passage of time marks the difference between yesterday's heroes and tomorrow's.

Still, not willing to be left alone at the altar, Montana's *Gardiner Wonderland* joined the *Union* in its cacophony of critical assessments of Martha Jane's life, heralding her death with the headline, "Calamity Jane Finally Does the Proper Thing." The Montana newspaper, *The White Sulphur Springs Meagher Republican*, wrote an even harsher critique, urging readers to consider the facts of Calamity's life: "'Calamity Jane,' as she was vulgarly and perhaps appropriately called, was a notorious prostitute who had lived in every town of the state as long as the citizens would allow her to." He went on to say that she consorted with "roughs, rogues, rounders, robbers and highwaymen," and "her natural haunts were in the red light or bad land districts."

He neglected to explain to his readers that, with the history of her parents thrust upon her, young Martha Jane couldn't possibly have expected to turn out to be Queen Victoria. Add to that the ignominious manner in which she was dumped into society, and the analogy becomes even more ridiculous.

That same editor continued, condemning Calamity for never having served as a scout and, in fact, having earned her notoriety solely by drinking "bad whiskey" and using "obscene, boisterous and indecent language." Condemning the adulation of Martha in the newspapers, the editor concluded, "If the press of the state cannot find a more respectable person to eulogize through its columns for the delectation of its respectable readers, better that it 'pi' its forms, throw its presses in the dump pile and embark in the cultivation of rattlesnakes."

Again, this same narrow-minded writer neglected to recognize that Martha's thirst for "obscene" language was part of her aura, as well as her defense. Not many "men" in the Old West avoided the challenges Martha faced, so how could a woman thrust into performing equally and fittingly well (sometimes known as "surviving") have done any differently?

Regardless of the printed clatter, not even the most venomous attacks against Martha Jane's persona could sway the affection that the American public felt for her. As the *Belle Fourche Bee* observed only a few days after her funeral, Martha "was buried beside 'Wild Bill' Hickok, one of her old consorts, in the cemetery at Deadwood, and now Deadwood will have a second attraction to exhibit to visitors from the east."

And the rest, as they say, is history.

CHAPTER FIFTEEN

On Death and Dying

'*Calamity Jane' Is Dead;*
Who Became Famous as an Indian Fighter.
Wearing Men's Clothes She Served with Gens. Custer and Miles
Most Picturesque Character in the West.

—THE *NEW YORK TIMES*

CALAMITY JANE'S OBITUARY, MUCH LIKE THE WOMAN HERSELF, WAS straightforward, matter-of-fact, and to a great extent a canard. Let's not be mistaken: Martha was no fool. She knew exactly what she had to do from an early age to survive in a cold, cruel, hard world leveraged against her. Her bravado was never for show or self-aggrandizement as much as it was for survival. Her drinking was a culmination of a desire to "fit in" with the men around her and to be accepted by her peers, as well as a panacea for the pain she had endured throughout her life. Her cursing and spitting and smoking big black cigars and dressing like a man and shooting and riding and bull whacking all concealed the ultimate woman inside, the female and very feminine heart and soul of a person who just happened to wear the name Calamity. To that extent, she was truly an extraordinary woman who had to struggle her entire life against the male-engendered egos and antifeminism so prevalent in the day. Otherwise, she would have perished—and what remained of her family, her beloved siblings, would have perished right along with her.

There's no other way around it.

Her obituary said in summation what every man, woman, and child Martha had ever befriended believed about her intrinsically.

"CALAMITY JANE" GOES
"OVER THE RANGE"

Death of the Woman Scout, Mining Camp Nurse and Pioneer Character.

The Sioux Falls, South Dakota, **Daily Argus-Leader**

Deadwood. Aug. 2—Calamity Jane, perhaps the most noted female character who ever "came down the pike," or figured in the life of the frontier, died at the mining camp of Terry Saturday afternoon after an illness lasting sometime, though she had been confined to her bed only a few days. She had been a familiar figure in the mining camps of the Hills country since 1870 and was probably known by sight by more people than any other pioneer character in the West.

In the days when the life in the camps was known as "wild and woolly" Calamity Jane was in her glory, and to the day of her death she carried as her passport to favor messages from the heads of departments of this government acknowledging gratitude for services rendered on the plains and in the Hills as a scout, an occupation usually reserved for men, but which she performed with singular bravery and fidelity. She was clever, fearless, daring and could shoot as readily as she could swear and in both lines she was proficient, but there is many an old timer who remembers when she could also perform the deeds of mercy in a sick room or camp where women hardly ever ventured and ladies never.

With all her eccentricities which have seemed more pronounced as pioneer customs have passed away, she retained her friends in generous numbers while she has for several years divided her time between the mining towns of South Dakota and Montana she was warmly welcomed on her return here where she had passed so much of her life.

*The real name of "Calamity Jane" was Jane Burke, her last hus-
band being Clinton Burke. She has a married daughter who lives in
North Dakota and the dead woman spent considerable of her time the
last remaining years of her life traveling about from the Hills to the
place where her daughter lives and from there to Montana and back
again as the inclination came over her. In her travels she always rode
in the smoking car and usually carried with her a box of cigars and
sometimes a little liquid for the stomach's sake.*

*By her request the remains will lie buried by the pioneers of the
Black Hills beside the resting place of "Wild Bill" (Hickok) her former
consort, in Mt. Moriah cemetery in Deadwood.*

It's an interesting commentary that one of America's first suffragettes—
and by far its most outspoken and least glamorous—led such an amaz-
ingly complicated, painful, and self-destructive life. As Dora DuFran
argued in looking back over how Calamity's tragic and unfortunate
beginnings shaped her later life, even good women "brought up with
every protection from the evils of the world and with good associations"
were likely to replicate their upbringings as adults. But Calamity had no
such protective origins as "good women"; she grew up the "product of the
wild and woolly West. She was not immoral; but unmoral. . . . With her
upbringing, how could she be anything but . . . ?"

Like M. L. Fox's notable account of Calamity in Deadwood in
1895/96, DuFran's postmortem of Calamity's brief, meteoric rise through
life provided another feminine perspective on the unique nature of the
woman. It, too, exuded feelings of sisterhood and empathy missing from
so many of the masculine-driven accounts of Calamity Jane. DuFran,
having promised to take care of Calamity's grave, paid for a sculpture to
be placed on it, a sculpture that the town of Deadwood maintains to this
day. And on Calamity's gravestone are carved these few words:

*Mrs. M. E. Burke CALAMITY JANE Died Aug. 1, 1903 Aged 53
YRS.*

How ironic that, in the very town that Calamity most considered "home," the place where she chose to be eternally interred, from which she departed so often and returned one final time—how very ironic that the engravers misspelled her name on her tombstone. They even got her age wrong. But that would not have been something to upset the "old girl." Such erroneous information about her—whether self-induced or by the result of the fertile imaginations of dime novelists and spread across the universe by the working press—had plagued the life and times of Calamity Jane nearly from her birth. Who would have expected anything different in her death?

When I initially set out to write a book nearly a decade ago about another western legend, John Henry "Doc" Holliday—the book he had always wanted written, the story of the *real* John Henry, the untarnished, unvarnished truth about the man—I formed an immediate kinship with him. By the end of the book that concluded with Doc's passing, I felt as if I had just laid to rest my very own brother. That's the strength of the bonds that Doc had on those few people he called *friends*, as well as on those who knew him from outside his small inner circle looking in.

In a way, Martha Jane Cannary—Calamity Jane—was the female antithesis of Doc Holliday. Nowhere near alike in education or manners, worlds apart in culture, beyond comparable in attire and comportment and temperament, the two had a couple very obvious traits in common. One was a deadly accuracy with their six-guns and a willingness to display it whenever called upon. The other was an indomitable spirit and genuine love for humanity despite their having been dealt a hard blow in life—with many more such obstacles to follow.

Like Doc, Jane was affable enough, quick to smile, and yet guarded against all the elements, human and otherwise, that might set themselves against her. Like Doc, Jane drank to excess to drown her fears, sorrows, and pain and succeeded . . . in time. And, like Doc, Jane paid the ultimate price: She died far too early for the person of stout heart and immeasurable goodwill that she proved to be.

So the two, in my mind, are kindred spirits, linked inexorably by the commonality of their goals. The first was to provide aid and comfort to their fellow human beings who were suffering in life through no cause of their own. The second was to leave behind in their legacies as little harshness and bitterness to their fellow travelers as humanly possible. Toward that end, it appears to me that both succeeded admirably.

While Doc Holliday had his lifelong paramour and soulmate, Big Nose Kate, to travel with him throughout the West, ready and willing to provide warmth, succor, and support for the man she undoubtedly loved, Jane had a cadre of people whose own feelings toward her might not have been so universally unconditional. Her mother, her father, her baby brother Cy, her sister, Lena, Martha's husband Clinton Burke and their daughter, Jessie. Oh, yes, and Lige.

Lige.

Elijah Cannary. Her baby brother.

Elijah, the one person on earth for whom she felt most responsible and proudest as he grew from a small boy to early manhood. The one in whom she saw the most promise. The one who could read and write and think and set his goals and meet and actually exceed them. The one toward whom she felt the most maternal.

But soon after Lige left the Borner ranch for good, he fell in with some bandits. Some historians allege they included LeRoy Parker—better known as Butch Cassidy—and his legendary Hole in the Wall Gang, consisting of Butch, Harry Longabaugh (the Sundance Kid), William Carver, Ben Kilpatrick, and Harvey Logan (Kid Curry). When Martha Jane learned that Lige was apprehended for a host of crimes, not the least of which was horse stealing, she was heartbroken. When she heard that he had been convicted and sentenced to a year of hard labor at the Laramie Territorial Prison, she was devastated. By then, she was too feeble, too sickly, and too poor to make the trek west to see her baby brother even one last time. And her heart must have been shattered into a billion shards of glass at that realization. She must have suspected as the courts locked him away that she would never see him again.

And so she took to drink once more. And to still heavier drink. And to still more, until the numbness she felt turned out to be far preferable to the tearing of her heart at the loss of her brother. Still, looking at things from the outside in, some might wonder if she couldn't have found a reason to go on the wagon, to forsake the dreaded dregs of alcoholism in exchange for a physically healthier way through life? Couldn't she have found the inner *strength*?

If so, I don't know how; for Martha endured the pain she was dealt from early on until her final days on earth. It was an inexhaustible, agonizing pain that—like the lifelong battle with tuberculosis that faced down Doc, consuming him little by little, one day at a time, one moment after another—spurred on Martha's own anguish.

And when Martha died, just as in Doc's passing, the world became a little smaller, and the inheritance she had gifted to the western plains and valleys she traversed for decades was suddenly gone forever.

Martha Jane Cannary stood as a genuine western hero—a symbol of all that is good in America and in the American people. She was the very essence of the West. Was she as pure as the driven snow over the Grand Tetons in the middle of January? Hardly. Was she as honest as the day that stretches out its shadows along the lakes and rivers of central Montana? Not likely. But she was brave to the point of being foolhardy. She was compassionate to the point of being reckless. And she was devoted to the point of no return. Stack those attributes up against the omnipresent sting of pain plaguing her throughout her life, and it's a wonder she did a good deed or had a decent thought ever. For all her goodness, her big heart, and her warmth for her fellow passengers through life, she suffered the continual nonstop ragging, nagging aches of life.

And virtually everyone who knew her realized it.

As Dora DuFran—her acquaintance, friend, and sometime employer—said so astutely years after Martha's demise:

Her funeral was one of the largest in the history of Deadwood. She is buried in Mt. Moriah which overlooks the city which she had helped when Calamity rode the passes. She is buried near the grave of Wild Bill, one of her old time pals.

The tall pines sound as if sighing. The old timers she worked with are all around her. After life's fitful fever, she sleeps well. The ancients believed iron could be transmuted into gold. This woman of iron was needed in the structure of the West. Her heart was of pure, precious gold. Her deeds have earned her the right to walk the Golden Streets.

The Master understands, and Calamity most surely has her reward. The charitable deeds have turned the buckskin suit into a robe of white. If she retains her old ego, a horse would be preferable to wings.

And just who are we who walk the earth and experience the excitement and relive the joys and vitality of the life of one of America's most remarkable pioneers? Who are we to doubt it?

As Calam herself used to say when she bellied up to the bar and slammed her fist down against the hard oaken boards, "Give me a shot of booze, and slop 'er over the brim!"

Bibliography

Bennett, Estelline. *Old Deadwood Days.* 1928. Reprint, Lincoln: University of Nebraska Press, 1982.

Biography.com. (2017). *Calamity Jane* [online]. Available at: https://www.biography .com/people/calamity-jane-9234950 [accessed August 12, 2016].

Calamities of Calamity Jane, The, HistoryNet. (2010). *HistoryNet.* Retrieved February 1, 2017, from http://www.historynet.com/the-calamities-of-calamity-jane.htm.

Calamity Jane. (2017). *Cowgirls.com.* Retrieved September 28, 2016, from http://www .cowgirls.com/dream/cowgals/calamity.htm.

Calamity Jane. (2017). *Deadwoodmagazine.com.* Retrieved February 9, 2017, from http:// www.deadwoodmagazine.com/archivedsite/Archives/Girls_Calamity.htm.

Calamity Jane: Rowdy Woman of the West. (2017). *Legendsofamerica.com.* Retrieved April 10, 2017, from http://www.legendsofamerica.com/we-calamityjane.html.

Calamity Jane is born, C. (2017). *Calamity Jane is born—May 01, 1852. HISTORY.com.* Retrieved August 23, 2016, from http://www.history.com/this-day-in-history/ calamity-jane-is-born.

Cerney, Jan. *Calamity Jane and Her Siblings: The Saga of Lena and Elijah Canary* [*sic*]. Charleston, SC: History Press, 2016.

Discover the History of the Real Deadwood, South Dakota. (2017). *Deadwood.com.* Retrieved May 10, 2017, from https://www.deadwood.com/history/?gclid= CjwKEAjwiLDMBRDF586Bwe2Sq3.

DuFran, Dora. *Low Down on Calamity Jane.* Edited by Helen Rezatto. Reprint. Stickney, SD: Argus Printers, 1981.

Etulain, Richard W. *The Life and Legends of Calamity Jane.* Norman, OK: University of Oklahoma Press, 2014.

Faber, Doris. *Calamity Jane: Her Life and Her Legend.* New York, NY: Houghton Mifflin, 1992.

[Fox, M. L.] "Calamity Jane." *Illustrated American* (7 March 1896): 312.

Freeman, Lewis R. *Down the Yellowstone.* New York: Dodd & Company, 1922.

McLaird, James D. *Calamity Jane: The Woman and the Legend.* Norman, OK: University of Oklahoma Press, 2012.

Sollid, Roberta Beed. *Calamity Jane.* Helena, MT: Montana Historical Society Press, 1995.

Thomson, David. (2004). "The Truth about Calamity Jane." *The Independent*. Retrieved August 10, 2017, from http://www.independent.co.uk/arts-entertainment/films/features/the-truth-about-calamity-jane-550827.html.

User, S. (2017). *Calamity Jane: The Wild West. Thewildwest.org*. Retrieved February 6, 2017, from http://www.thewildwest.org/cowboys/wildwestlegendarywomen/199-calamityjane.

NEWSPAPERS

Anaconda (MT) *Standard*
Baltimore American
Belle Fourche (SD) *Bee*
Big Horn (NY) *Sentinel*
Billings (MT) *Daily Gazette*
Billings (MT) *Post*
Billings (MT) *Times*
Billings (MT) *Weekly Register Call*
Black Hills (SD) *Daily Times*
Black Hills (SD) *Union*
Buffalo Enquirer
Buffalo Morning Express
Butte (MT) *Miner*
Cheyenne Daily Leader
Cheyenne Tribune
Chicago Daily Inter-Ocean
Daily Argus (SD) *Leader*
Deadwood (SD) *Evening Independent*
Deadwood (SD) *Pioneer-Times*
Denver Post
Fergus County (MT) *Argus*
Freemont (CO) *Clipper*
Gardiner (MT) *Wonderland*
Hot Springs (SD) *Weekly Star*
Jamestown (ND) *Daily Alert*
Klondike (AK) *Nugget*
Laramie (WY) *Daily Boomerang*
Laramie (WY) *Statesman*
Lead (WY) *Daily Call*
Lead (SD) *Evening Call*
Lewistown (MT) *Democrat*
Livingston (MT) *Post*
London Star
Mandan (ND) *Pioneer*
Minneapolis Star
Montana Post

New York Weekly
New York World
Oakes (ND) *Republican*
Ogden (UT) *Standard*
Rapid City (SD) *Daily Journal*
Red Lodge (MT) *Picket*
Rocky Mountain (CO) *Daily News*
Rocky Mountain (CO) *Herald*
Sheridan (WY) *Post*
Sioux Falls (SD) *Argus Leader*
Sioux Falls (SD) *Press*
St. Paul (MN) *Dispatch*
Star Valley (WY) *Independent*
Sundance (WY) *Gazette*
Terry (SD) *News-Record*
Thermopolis (WY) *Independent*
Uinta (UT) *Chieftain*
White Sulphur Springs (MT) *Meagher Republican*
Wind River (WY) *Mountaineer*
Wyoming State Tribune

About the Author

Born and raised in Chicago, **D. J. Herda** worked for years at the *Chicago Tribune*, as well as at numerous other Chicago-area newspapers and magazines, before becoming an internationally syndicated columnist. During its decade-long run, Herda's column, "In Focus," appeared in more than 1,100 newspapers with a combined circulation of nearly twenty million readers. As a syndicated photo and travel columnist, he developed strong ties to the editorial department of every major newspaper in North America, from the *Washington Post* to the *Los Angeles Times*, and sends out interviews, backgrounders, review copies, etc., for both himself and for the client authors he represents as an editor/ghostwriter/book doctor.

Herda's interest in western Americana goes back to his childhood. He has published on the subjects of Doc Holliday, Frank and Jesse James, Billy the Kid, Butch Cassidy and the Wild Bunch, Wyatt Earp, and other western legends. He has written "Forts of the American West" and other articles for *American West*, *Arizona Highways*, and other magazines. His fascination with Calamity Jane stretches back to his earliest recollections, and he has been researching her life for decades, convinced that one day he would chronicle the story of the *real* Martha Jane Cannary in a book. D. J. Herda has lived in the Rocky Mountains of the southwestern United States for nearly three decades.